POINT ME TO THE SKIES

JESSICA LYNN JACQUEZ

Copyright © 2020 by Jessica Lynn Jacquez.

All rights reserved. Printed in the United States of America. No part of this book may be used or reproduced in any manner whatsoever without prior written permission of Jessica Lynn Jacquez. Some names and identifying details have been changed to protect the privacy of individuals.

Cover Design: Ebook Launch

Editor: Sarah Fox at The Bookish Fox

1st edition.

ISBN 978-0-578-61668-1 (Paperback)
ISBN 978-0-578-61669-8 (Digital)

Scripture quotations are from the Holy Bible, New International Version®. NIV® Copyright © 1973, 1978, 1984, 2011 by Biblica, Inc.™ Used by permission of Zondervan. All rights reserved worldwide. www.zondervan.com. The "NIV" and "New International Version" are trademarks registered in the United States Patent and Trademark Office by Biblica, Inc.™

To God—my Savior and Comforter.
How grateful I am to be known and loved by You.

To my husband, David — my biggest fan.
You've always believed in me.
Your patience and support made this book possible.

To my brother, Paul — my first best friend.
I don't know what I would have done without you.

To my mother, Lureen — I couldn't be prouder of you.
I love you.

Introduction

Growing up, my job was simply to survive. There was no time spent planning for the future or entertaining thoughts of college or which career I wanted to get into when I was older. But I knew one thing: I desperately wanted to reach those that felt broken and beaten down by the world. The ones that were lonely and searching, like I was.

I didn't write this book because I found every answer I was looking for. I did, however, find peace. My story is laden with mistakes, both on my end and the end of those around me, and many of the things in this book were difficult to write about, but that's how I knew I was writing about the right things. I believe that we can help one another the most by being honest about the struggles we face, and when we finally tell the truth, we begin to heal.

My hope with sharing this story is to show others that our pasts don't have to define us and although we carry scars, we don't have to carry shame.

I've done my best to tell this story as accurately as possible. Every incident written about indeed took place; however, there are incidences in this story where the order of those events are questionable and after spending far too much time trying to get these details in the perfect order, I decided I'd write the events in the order I truly believed was likely, along with looking to close friends and family to corroborate my story to give the most accurate account.

Chapter 1

I was five years old sitting in my grandfather's tattered gray recliner in the corner of the living room. Tears poured down my cheeks as I sat stiff with my hands folded tightly on my lap.

"Where is your mother!" my grandmother screamed as she stood in front of me.

Her face was red from crying, and her teeth and lips were stained from the jug of red wine she had been drinking that morning. I kept my eyes down toward the floor as she stepped closer; I could see her feet standing in front of me. She bent down until her face was next to mine, and then she screamed at me. I could feel her breath on my face. She stomped down the hall back to her bedroom and slammed the door shut.

I cried quietly, careful not to make noise. I could hear yelling coming from her bedroom. Then there was silence.

Just then, I heard the clink of the metal doorknob hit the wall. I looked up to see her charging toward me again.

I looked up at her. Her watery eyes glistened from the streak of light peeking through the curtain. She had cried and sobbed and screamed all morning.

"I hate you!" she shrieked.

I looked at the floor. Tears flowed from my eyes onto my legs.

"Where's Lureen?! I want you out of my house!" she shouted before storming back down the hall and once again slamming the bedroom door shut.

The apartment was kept dark. The lights were off, and the blinds were closed, casting a gloomy gray feeling into the room. On the wall a few feet from me was the black call box. When my mother arrived, I'd have to use it to let her into the apartment. I rocked back and forth in the recliner as I stared anxiously at the box, waiting for it to ring. I worried that I wouldn't be tall enough to reach the box to let her in so I tiptoed over to it to check. I stood tall and reached my fingers as high as I could, but I couldn't reach. At the sound of an abrupt noise coming from my grandmother's bedroom, I quickly returned to the chair. I leaned back in the old chair and closed my eyes while I waited for my mother. Suddenly, there she was, coming through the front door.

"Get your stuff and let's go," she whispered.

"Mom! How did you get in?"

"A neighbor buzzed me in. Now let's go before she hears us."

She snatched my pink Barbie backpack from the couch and motioned me to head toward the door. With her hand on my back, she gently pushed me out of the apartment and softly closed the door behind her. She gripped my hand, and our feet moved as quickly as they could down the stairs.

"I don't know why Grandma's mad at me," I said, worried.

"It's okay, Jess. Don't worry about her."

We reached the bottom of the stairs. My father and three-year-old brother, Paul, were waiting in the car.

"Todd!" my mother shouted as we approached the car. Dad hopped out of the passenger seat to push his seat forward and let me in.

"We're goin' to Castro Valley Emergency."

I paused and looked at them.

"Are we going to the hospital?" I asked from the backseat.

"We're gonna have the doctors check you. Nothin' you need to worry about," she said as she shifted the car into reverse.

Within a few minutes, we arrived at the emergency room. With my hand in hers, my mother and I rushed across the parking lot toward the entrance. My legs could hardly keep up with hers. The electric double doors slid open.

"Go sit down!"

I took a seat in the brightly lit waiting area while my mother talked to the receptionist. My father and Paul sat next to me as we waited. None of us said much to one another as we waited for my name to be called.

"Jessica!" the nurse shouted from the doorway in front of us.

We all got up quickly and followed her down the hall. Once inside the examination room, Mom and Dad signaled the nurse to step aside with them.

"Jessica was at my parents overnight and … my father was seen coming out of Jessica's room."

I *did* remember my grandfather standing above my bed early that morning. He was in his boxers. I pretended to be sleeping, but as I rolled over, I opened my eyes just enough to see him standing there. Although, I truly didn't remember anything else happening. After speaking to my parents, the nurse came over to me, pulled the curtain closed, and asked me to take off everything but my underwear.

"He did this same thing to Kara. Messed her up till this day," I could hear Mom say. "I never thought I'd have to worry about him around my own daughter."

"What a disgrace," Dad replied, then both of them left the room.

I stripped down to my underwear and waited. The room was cold, and I could hear the white paper crinkle underneath me as

I fidgeted on the bench. A couple of minutes later, the doctor entered the room and pulled his chair up next to me.

"Hi, Jessica. I'm Dr. Thomas. We're gonna do a little check up on you, okay? It will only take a minute."

"Okay," I replied timidly.

I lay back on the cold examination table and peered at the ceiling while the doctor began his examination. Several uncomfortable minutes later, it was over, and I was told that I could get dressed. I wondered how this experience was any better than the one they feared I had with my grandfather.

I put my clothes back on and anxiously waited to be told I could leave. I sat under the harsh white lights and wondered when my parents would come into the room. Finally, my father, holding Paul in his arms, opened the door and signaled for me to come out while he and my mother were finishing up a conversation with the doctor.

"Well, thank you, doctor," she said as she glanced down in my direction.

"Yes, thank you so much," my father said as he reached out to shake the doctor's hand.

"Alright, Jess, let's get goin,'" Mom said. She reached for my hand, and the four of us made our way down the long hallway, through the double doors, and back to the parking lot.

No one spoke to each other as we all loaded into the car, even Paul was quiet as he was placed in his car seat. The only sound was that of the seatbelts clicking into place.

I looked out of the window at the sun shining through the tall tree next to us. Then Mom turned the car around and we headed toward the exit. Dad gently placed his arm around her shoulders and I began to hear the sound of her crying.

"My own father ... I never thought I'd have to worry about him abusing his own granddaughter," she said under her breath.

I wanted to ask questions about what had happened, but I knew when to be quiet. I watched from the backseat as Dad comforted her. He rubbed her neck as he assured her that everything would be okay.

Chapter 2

The four of us lived in a small trailer on 168th Avenue in San Leandro. The trailer was twenty-seven feet long, and every inch of it could be seen from the fold out bed that my brother and I shared.

Next to our bed was the kitchen where there was a small collapsible table where we ate our meals. Just a few feet down the narrow hallway was Mom and Dad's bedroom. It was just large enough to fit a bed and a small television on top of the built-in dresser. The only privacy was behind the flimsy accordion-style door that closed off Mom and Dad's bedroom from the rest of the trailer.

Paul and I were raised to be tough. We were brought up in a family where seatbelts were optional, yellow traffic lights meant go faster, and where car rides consisted of Dad's cigarette ashes flying into our faces from the front seat. It was ridiculous to believe in Santa so Mom and Dad never allowed it. They did, however, believe in loyalty. It was their code of honor, and the precept they proudly lived by. "All you have is your word" and "Be loyal, and don't be a snitch" were the rules they taught to Paul and me. When Mom's friend, Jackie, needed clean pee for an upcoming drug test, I was sent into the bathroom to produce it for her. Or when Dad's friend Stormy needed a place to stay while he was trying to get sober, we folded down our kitchen table and made a bed for him.

Mom and Dad fought quite a bit, and the two of them hurling things at one another occurred a few times a week. I never knew when a quiet evening would suddenly turn into a violent brawl. Mom's drinking and anger were mostly to blame. Despite this, Mom and Dad decided to take off to Lake Tahoe and finally get married.

Despite the arguing being a normal occurrence, there were seemingly calm days in between the dysfunction and chaos. And Mom had moments that she was fun. There were days when she'd open up every window, rain or shine, and sing along to her Tom Petty cassette while cleaning the house. Paul and I would each find something to clean too, knowing that afterward, if we were good, she'd bake something for us. When we were done, the scent of Pine Sol and fresh baked chocolate chip cookies, or one of her famous banana pudding cakes, filled the house.

My mother was beautiful with her strawberry blonde hair and striking blue-green eyes. She radiated strength, and you recognized that as soon as she looked at you. She was forceful, yet fragile, all at the same time. And she had a way of being silly and childlike. Like when it was raining, she'd plow the car through every big puddle she spotted as we drove. We'd watch the water crash over our car like a huge wave while she giggled from the front seat. Deep down, Mom was just a kid herself.

Even in my earliest memories, Mom and I didn't have the typical mother-daughter relationship. She spoke to me as if I were her only friend, and I think that I was. She didn't talk to me like I was a child; she spoke to me the way someone does to a therapist.

During many of our car rides together, she shared stories of her past relationships and how they damaged her, her regrets of never graduating high school, or about the time she was raped by two boys under the bleachers at Tennyson High. Or the most painful of all, her grief over losing custody of her first son, my estranged older brother.

It was 1986, three years before I would be born, and Mom was living in her car with Jeremy, who was three years old at the time. Jeremy's father was a heroin addict who beat her regularly, so in an effort to escape, she took Jeremy and left. With nowhere else to go, the two of them lived in her car and ate the food that strangers left behind at fast food restaurants. Finally, Child Protective Services found out about their living situation, and they took Jeremy from her and sent him off to Oregon to live with his father's relatives. Eight years went by before they allowed her to speak to him again. Mom usually became very quiet after talking about this.

Although I couldn't have been more than six years old at the time, it didn't seem strange to me that she would tell me these things. I was happy she did. It felt like she trusted me and that I was her best friend, and she was mine. There was nothing she couldn't tell me. I loved her more than anything, and I understood, even then, that my mother needed someone to talk to.

During one car ride home, I remember looking up at her as she told me stories about a man who was the worst to her. I knew by her voice that she hated him. His name was John, and my mother spoke of him as if he were the rottenest man that she had ever known.

I listened closely as she told me how he'd come home after a night of drinking and beat her, sometimes until she lost consciousness. They lived in Fremont, California in a small trailer with broken windows and no electricity. Mom used whatever she could to block the cold air from coming inside, and when it was dark, she lit candles for light. Late one night, she said, John came home angry. She tried to calm him, but instead, he screamed at her, calling her names and telling her that she was worthless. He then reached for the leather belt around his waist. He unbuckled it, ripped it off his jeans, and swung it at her. He swung the belt so hard that the metal prong on the buckle pierced through her scalp. She told me that she could still recall the sensation of the metal prong being ripped out of her skin as he drew the belt back. Blood rushed, coagulating in her blonde hair.

"Then he went to bed," she said.

She then paused for a moment as if she were suddenly reliving the pain.

"I waited a few minutes until I could hear him snoring. Then I got off the floor and cleaned myself up," she said.

Shivers went down my spine as I listened to her tell this story that I would never be able to forget.

"That's why I'm so happy to be with your dad," she turned to me and said. "He treats me better than any other man I've ever known." She smiled, and I could see all of the pain melt right off of her at the thought of my father. I turned and looked quietly out of the window as she drove us the rest of the way home.

I loved my mom more than anything and hearing these stories was the reason I could never tell her the secrets I knew about my father.

The truth was that my mother had accused my grandfather of the very things my father was already doing to me. The earliest memory that I can recall was around my fifth birthday. After Mom and Paul were asleep, he climbed under my covers and laid next to me while he removed my nightgown. My heart pounded, and I pretended to be asleep because I didn't know what else to do. He then grabbed my hand and put it inside his boxers. My body was paralyzed, but my mind entered a place of uncontrollable anxiousness. The next ten minutes were the longest of my life.

When he was finally finished with me, he got up and walked back to his bedroom. I heard the sound of the door being pulled shut, and I felt like I could suddenly breathe again. I lay in bed for what felt like hours before I was able to fall asleep that night. The next morning, when I awoke, my father's visit was the very first thing I thought about. I kept my head under the covers, pretending to still be sleeping. I was too embarrassed to look my father in the eyes. I felt different after that night. Like something within me had changed, like I was no longer who I was before, and I was never able to get my mind out of that place of uneasiness and worry. I became insecure and anxious constantly, and I began to suffer from migraines often.

But as my mother told me the stories of the horrible men that mistreated her and beat her before she met my father, I knew that I never wanted her to be hurt again and that I would keep these secrets forever if I had to.

I spent a lot of time alone and in my thoughts. I enjoyed solitude because it was where I felt the most at peace. As the days went on, I spent more and more time alone, no longer wanting to go outside or play with the neighborhood kids. I stayed in the house and wrote poetry or drew pictures. Mom and Dad would even tease me about being a homebody, but what they didn't know was that being alone was where my mind felt the most at ease.

I avoided being alone with my father. He looked at me differently when others weren't around; it was the same way I saw him look at my mother. I avoided making eye contact because his long stares made me feel naked in front of him. When no one else was around, he showed affection toward me. He'd ask me for hugs, and when I hesitated because of how uncomfortable I was, he would ask me why I didn't love him. This made me feel guilty, and often left me feeling confused on how I was supposed to feel about my father.

Mom would always tell us what a great dad Paul and I had, and she'd remind us of the sacrifices he made to put food on the table and a roof over our heads. Dad was a mechanic, which was apparent from his calloused and grease-stained hands that never became clean. He worked long hours at the shop, and I don't remember him ever complaining about it.

We were reminded constantly to be grateful for what we had and to respect both of them for all they did for us. This also contributed to my conflicted emotions toward my father. And aside from the sexual abuse I secretly experienced, Dad was adored by everyone who knew him. He was known as charismatic and down-to-earth. He could make anyone laugh, and often I hated that I, too, laughed at his jokes. My mother was enamored with him. She loved his tattoos and his blue eyes. She often bragged about what a handsome and charming guy our father was. She told us how lucky we were to be his children.

Though she shared her most personal memories with me, my mother wasn't the nurturing, affectionate type, but I believed it was because she didn't know how to be, except with my father. Once in a while, however, there were moments that she was.

"I love your little moons," she'd say to me sweetly.

She said that I smiled so big that my eyes turned into sparkling, little crescent moons.

There were times of composure and calm. Times when the arguing paused, when the haunting memories of Dad's visit the night before were put aside momentarily, and when my anxiety and obsessive thoughts were dormant long enough to feel like we were a normal family.

One summer, we took day trips to Half Moon Bay almost every other weekend. It was only about an hour drive for us, but, a couple times, we stayed overnight. We brought blankets and parked our truck right near the beach. Mom loved the idea of waking up to the sound of the ocean. But even with all four of us sleeping together under the camper shell of Dad's truck, one night Dad crawled over to me and removed my pants. My mother was right next to me. I'm sure by the shallow breathing and the heavy beating of my heart, he knew that I was awake.

After that summer, most days were full of constant anger and drunkenness, punctuated with mom's fleeting moments of gentleness. Tenderness from my mother was short-lived, but it had a way of making up for all of her faults. It brought humanity back for just a moment and reminded me of how much I loved her.

Chapter 3

Within another year, things changed. Perhaps our family had been on a road of gradual decline for a while, but I remember it feeling like a swift change from what I was used to. Mom drank much more heavily than she did before, and the constant arguing between her and my father was much more violent. Now when Mom became upset or depressed, she threatened to kill herself. I can remember times I was called into her room when she was drunk.

"Jessica! Get in here right now!" she'd yell from her bed.

I would walk nervously down the hall. "Yes?" I asked politely.

"You know why I'm still in bed? Cause I'm so sick of you and your brother not keeping your damn toys picked up! If you loved me, you'd listen to me! Would you be happier if I just wasn't here anymore, huh? Would you be happy if I just slit my damn throat?"

"No, Mom. I'm sorry," I'd say as tears filled my eyes.

"Get outta my face, and go clean up your mess."

I quickly cleaned up my toys and anything else I could find that was messy.

One afternoon, after I was picked up from school, Mom and Dad began arguing in the car. The arguments between them normally started because my mother never felt good enough. She had been told in her past by her father, classmates, and exes that she was worthless and unintelligent so she was highly sensitive to anyone or anything that pointed out those insecurities or made her feel that way.

"Lureen, chill out!" Dad shouted from the passenger seat. I watched from the backseat as my mother turned to him, fuming with anger.

"I swear to God I will wreck this car with all of us in it!" she said to him.

"Mom, don't!" I cried out.

"You shut up!" she yelled at me.

Paul and I sat quietly in the backseat as profanities were shouted back and forth.

Suddenly, as the yelling reached its loudest, the car tires screeched as my mother slammed on the breaks.

"Get out of the car right now!" she shouted.

Dad got out of the car, pushed his seat forward and told us to get out too. It was cold, and the sky was gloomy as we stood on the sidewalk in front of a small business we had driven past many times. I stared at my mother as she sat in the car, and I wondered what would happen next.

Suddenly, Mom pressed the gas pedal to the floor and used her beloved Camaro to charge through the chained and locked cyclone fence in front of us. The metal fence swung open and hit the wall behind it as her car barreled through it. I cried as I watched, and I screamed as the car made its way toward the brick building at the end of the driveway.

"Stop the car, Lureen!" my father screamed.

Then, to my relief, she did. I asked my father if she were okay, but before answering, he left Paul and I on the sidewalk to run to the car. We stood by watching, then seconds later, Paul and I followed behind him. Dad leaned inside the driver side window to talk to her. I could hear her crying.

Soon I began to hear whispers between the two of them of how much they loved one another. Dad's arms reached into the car and over Mom's neck as the two of them kissed. Within minutes, they had made up, and the only physical damage done was scratches in the paint and a dent to the front of the car.

I didn't understand my mother's reason for her doing what she did, but I was learning by now that she didn't need a reason. Many times all she wanted was a reaction, whether that be from our father or from Paul and me. Maybe she felt loved by watching us all worry about her. It worked. I worried about my mother constantly.

Not long after crashing our car into the fence, it seemed that my mother didn't want to be a mother anymore. She had no interest in keeping a clean house or cooking meals. She stayed in her room and drank Jack Daniels, and in between her naps, I could hear her crying throughout the day. Occasionally I'd sneak into her room to check on her.

"Get away from me!" she'd yell when she saw me peeking in her room.

I knew Mom had a good side to her, but sometimes it was hard to see it under all the liquor.

Due to my mother's downward spiral and rapidly increasing anger, there came a day unlike any of the others. Dad was out running errands with Paul, leaving me alone with Mom for the morning. I stood in the doorway of her bedroom as she spoke to me from her bed until I said something to upset her. She quickly threw the blankets off of her, vaulted out of her bed, and came toward me.

"You're evil. How dare you," she said slowly while clenching her teeth so only her lips moved.

I trembled as I walked slowly down the hallway. I walked backward to keep my eyes on her.

"I'm sorry!" I said.

I took several more steps back as she came toward me.

"You're gonna pay for that," she said.

She glared at me as she approached me. There wasn't anywhere for me to run, but in an attempt to get away from her, I darted to the right underneath our kitchen table.

"I'm so sick of you!" she screamed.

From underneath the table, I could see her waist down to her feet. I watched as she turned to the right, and then I heard her rip open one of the kitchen drawers. In her hand was a knife. She slammed the drawer shut, and I watched her feet slowly turn around. She took one step and bent down to peak at me under the table. We didn't say a word to one another. She remained still while glaring at me and seething with anger.

"What're you gonna do with the knife, Mom?" I asked her while tears filled the corners of my eyes.

Suddenly, she thrust the knife under the table toward me.

"Mom," I shrieked, "stop!"

Again, she lunged the knife toward me. I used my arms to squeeze my legs in as close as I could, trying to be missed by the blade.

"I'm sorry!" I cried out. I could feel the wall pressed firmly against my back. There was nowhere else for me to go.

She thrust the knife at me again, only this time raising her aim higher. I now watched the tip of the knife get recklessly lunged toward my face.

"You're finally gonna get what you deserve, you little slut!" she said as she let out a devilish laugh. She sounded like a witch. My mother was always scariest when she laughed this way. There was something about seeing me scared that she took pleasure in. I believed it was moments like these that made her feel powerful.

Then, Mom stood up. I watched her feet take a step to the left and then remain still. Suddenly, she began crying angrily.

"I hate you!" she repeated over and over, each time louder than the last.

Just then, I heard a thud above me as she thrust the knife down toward the edge of the table in a chopping motion. I could hear the blade slice through the plastic lining of the table and into the wood. Then I could hear the grunting sound she released when she used her strength to rip the blade back out. Next, she drew the knife upward and then back down again as if she were using an ax to chop wood. Between her crying and mine, I couldn't make out what she was saying. All I could hear was the sound of the knife hacking the table above me. I clasped my arms tightly to my bare legs, and my body shook. Snot poured from my nose and strands of my hair clung to my cheeks.

I watched her feet move slightly as she made her way around the front of the table. She raised her arm up, then I heard the chop once again. Her feet inched slowly to the right as she continued to drive the knife down into the wood. One or two more minutes passed as she made her way around the rest of the table; then she was done, and with a sigh of exhaustion, she tossed the knife into the kitchen sink. I could hear the steel blade hit the metal as she walked toward her bedroom and drew her door closed. I crawled to my bed, and after a few minutes, I began to quietly tidy up the coloring books and toys I had lying out. I began to clean every time my mother became upset.

For the rest of the morning, I watched television with the volume low as she stayed in her room.

Two hours later, Dad returned home. He and Paul stepped inside the trailer while I sat on the couch quietly. I wanted to tell Dad what happened, but I knew if I said anything, my mother would hear me. Dad noticed my silence and paused to look at me. I discreetly pointed over to the table. He took a few steps and looked down at it, then back at me. He frowned and mouthed the word "sorry," but even he knew to not say a word about it to my mother. During times like this, I felt like my father was my friend.

The next morning, when I sat up in my bed, one of the first things I could see were the gashes in the table across from me, a stark reminder of what happened the day before. Just then, I heard my mother's crying from her bedroom. I got up and looked out of the window to see that Dad's truck was already gone. Mom and Dad must've been arguing again. I wondered if it had anything to do with the table marks I had showed him.

I turned on the television, keeping the volume as low as I could; Paul was still asleep next to me, and I didn't want to upset Mom with the noise. Within just a few minutes, I heard my name called. A familiar feeling of dread came from the pit of my stomach. I nervously made my way down the hall.

"Morning, Mom," I greeted her.

"Jess, I need you to do me a favor," she said as she tossed me a long-sleeved flannel, "Put this on."

She reached into the drawer next to her and then put a handful of wadded money in my hand.

"I need you to pick something up for me."

"Okay." I was glad to do something for her and to feel like she and I were friends again.

"Go to CJ's house. He'll know what to give you."

CJ was a guy that lived in our trailer park whom she and my father had become good friends with. He came over to smoke weed quite a bit, and Mom joked that if she weren't with my father, she'd be with him. But he was nice to Paul and me so I liked him.

I took the short walk to the other end of the trailer park and arrived at his doorstep. I knocked on his door and waited. CJ, tall and covered from the neck down in tattoos, answered the door.

"Hey, Jess," he said, confused.

"Hi, CJ. My mom asked me to pick something up for her." I pulled out the wadded-up bills from my chest pocket.

He paused and stared at me. "What?" he asked, annoyed.

"My mom's in bed, and she asked me to come here for her."

He paused for a moment and then let out a loud sigh. He then reached his hand out to accept the money.

"Hold on," he said as he turned back into his trailer.

He turned back around and discreetly tucked a bag of weed in my flannel pocket.

"Tell your mom I'm never doin' this again."

"Okay," I said.

CJ shut his door, and I walked back.

Our parents had always been very open about their smoking. "It's good for your health, even though it might kill some brain cells," Mom and Dad would say, and they truly believed that. Whenever the four of us got in the car to go anywhere, Mom and Dad lit up a joint, and we'd drive to wherever it was we were going with our car full of smoke. When riding in our single cab truck, where Paul and I sat in-between them, they'd have Paul and I pass the joint back and forth for them. Mom told us that each time she got pregnant, she quit all the hard stuff, but she continued to smoke weed during all three of her pregnancies. She laughed as she credited it to why Paul and I were so smart. After all, I did make honor roll every year.

Minutes later, I returned home with Mom's weed, then sprawled out on the living room floor and colored yet another portrait of Strawberry Shortcake. Soon I began to hear mom's distinctive cough coming from her bedroom. I always preferred Mom's smoking over her drinking. Smoking didn't have the same negative effects on her mood the way that drinking usually did.

But shortly after this, I started seeing something new lying around the house. White powder lined up on a small mirror, then left on the bed, or on a countertop. It was cocaine. Up until that point, I had only ever seen it in movies. I wondered what kind of effects it would have on Mom's mood. Dad's mood, however, never changed.

One morning, while in second grade, I stood outside my classroom in line with all the other students. We were waiting for the bell to ring and for our teacher to open the door. It was cold that morning before we left the house so Mom had given me one of her flannels to put on over my long-sleeved shirt. She dropped me off at school, and as I waited in line, I noticed something in my pocket.

I reached my fingers inside, then felt something that caught my attention. Without pulling it out, I looked down into the pocket and saw a bag of weed. I tried to remain calm, but my heart raced, and I began to panic because I had seen police officers with dogs at my school recently. I was terrified that this would be the day the police and their dogs showed up again. I imagined them finding me and the drugs in my pocket, and I thought of what I would say. I knew if I told the truth, Mom and Dad would go to jail so that wasn't an option. I also knew that I couldn't throw it away because Mom and Dad would be mad.

All day, I stressed over what I would say if I got caught. My stomach was upset from worry, but I made it through the day without anyone finding out what was in my pocket. As soon as the bell rang, I walked as fast as I could. I couldn't wait to tell Mom what happened and give her back her flannel. I hopped inside the car and told her what happened.

"What!" she shouted, "I gotta tell your dad when he gets home!" She laughed as we drove away.

Chapter 4

Over the next year, I suffered from an overwhelming amount of anxiety and obsessive thoughts. I worried until it made me sick to my stomach or triggered a migraine. Mom and Dad had taken notice of the constant migraines and suggested I see a doctor, but I never did. The migraines persisted, happening sometimes several times a week. Many times a fun evening playing and wrestling with cousins ended in me lying on a bed in the dark, waiting for the pain to subside.

Soon, however, things would become even more difficult for me, and the physical symptoms I experienced would be exacerbated. After not working for a while, my mother got hired on as a cashier at the gas station down the road. It was the same gas station my father worked at during the day. She'd now be working night shifts, and with her new schedule, she wouldn't come home until midnight, or sometimes later.

With Mom being out of the house at night, it was easier for my father to do what he wanted, knowing that my mother wouldn't be home. His visits became more frequent. Every night that she was at work, I would be woken up by him. Sleep was not restful for me. I knew that shortly after falling asleep, I would wake up to my father in my bed, then I would lie awake for hours sometimes, long enough to hear when Mom's car pulled up to the house. But there were other times that my father would visit, and I wouldn't know. One morning, I awoke, and as I sat up rubbing my eyes, Mom stood in front of me and asked where my clothes were. I hadn't yet realized I was naked.

"What're you doin' sleepin' like that? Your brother sleeps right next to you," she said. I was embarrassed. I said nothing as I quickly searched under the blanket for my clothes.

My mother told me throughout my childhood that if a man ever hurt me or touched me, she would kill him.

"So you tell me if anyone ever touches you or makes you feel uncomfortable," she would say. "I'll kill anyone that harms my kids."

Mom was fired up when she said things like this, and I knew she meant every word. Even though she wasn't always the best example of what a mother should be, she'd be damned if anyone else treated her kids badly.

But this was another reason why I couldn't tell her. I believed her when she said she would kill someone. One thing I knew about Mom was she wasn't scared of going to jail; she had been there several times before.

Scenarios of me telling my mother about my dad played over and over in my mind, but so did the images of her going to prison. I worried that Paul, who slept just inches from me, would wake up one of these nights. And I feared there'd be a night when my mother would come home early from work only to find my father in my bed. Not a day passed that I did not think about these things.

One night after Paul had fallen asleep, I lay in bed watching television. I could see the light of the TV coming from my father's room, and I could hear a little tune that he was singing.

I turned back toward the television and continued watching my favorite nighttime show: *Mama's Family*. Suddenly, I could hear the tune he was singing get louder. He was walking out of his room, and soon he was standing at the edge of my bed.

He stood in front of me in a long burgundy robe my mother had gotten him for his birthday. The belt was left untied, leaving the robe wide open, exposing his naked body underneath. Embarrassed, I quickly looked back at the television.

"You didn't close the curtains all the way, Jess," he said while pointing up toward the curtains behind me.

I turned around to look. They were closed the same way they were each night. I looked back at the television.

"They look closed," I said while not looking at him.

"No, they're not. You don't want someone peekin' in here do ya?"

I kept my eyes on the television.

"Here, let me fix it." He sighed.

He lifted up his leg onto the bed, then reached forward to adjust the curtain.

"How's this?" he asked as his leg was stretched out in front of me.

"Fine," I said.

I turned my face away from him and back toward the TV. I felt his weight shift the bed as he stepped down onto the floor.

"Your mom should be home in a little while. You should get to sleep soon."

I knew once I shut off the television, he would be getting into my bed shortly after.

"I'm not tired yet. Can I stay up a little longer?"

"Uh." He hesitated. "Ten more minutes. That's it."

"Okay," I replied.

But I planned on keeping the television on for as long as I could. I thought maybe he would leave me alone if I just stayed awake. Every few minutes, I'd look down the hall and see the light shining from his TV until eventually he turned it off and went to bed. My plan had worked.

During my father's visits, my mind would drift off into imaginary places, and at times, my imagination ran so wild it was almost as if I had left my body. In those moments, I was gone, far away from anything that was happening to me. But often times, my mind would take me to the same place, one that I never understood: a large white room where I was all alone. There was no one and nothing there. No walls or windows and no doors for me to get out. Each time I found myself there, I walked around the room, looking for someone, or something, but I never found anyone or any way out. Once my father would leave my bed, sometimes I would stay in this white room or I would stare off at the blank screen of the television. Other times, I would quietly grab my cassette player and fall asleep listening to my favorite cassette: *The Greatest Hits by Patsy Cline*.

 I was eight years old, and, not knowing any better, I would lie awake at night convinced that I would soon become pregnant. I imagined that my belly would begin to grow, and that's when I would have to tell my mother everything that had been happening to me. I wondered how I'd explain myself and how angry she'd be with me.

 One Saturday morning, I found myself sitting in the passenger seat of our old white Chevy pickup. It was just me and my father, and we were on our way to the Oakland landfill. I stared out of the window and watched people as they passed us by. The ride was quiet, which was how I liked it. Then, Dad looked over at me and asked me a question. "Do you know why I come visit you at night?"

I could feel my heart beating out of my throat, and I felt my face and ears getting hot.

"No." I focused my gaze out of the passenger window, trying to be as removed from the conversation as possible.

"Well, I do it 'cause I love you," he said, "and it's for your own good. I'm checking you for boys. It's important."

I didn't know what any of this meant. My small, eight-year old-body sat stiff. My knuckles were white as I tried to hide the frustration within me.

"This isn't something we'll tell your mom about though." He turned to me and said, "she wouldn't understand."

I clenched my bare legs together and sat hunched over in an attempt to hide the shape of my undeveloped chest. It was where he often looked when he was speaking to me. I had learned to cower whenever in front of him. I slouched and shrunk myself in order to hide any feminine shape I thought my body may have had.

"And we shouldn't tell anyone else about it either, okay?"

I kept my face toward the window. "Okay."

I sat quietly in my blue jean skirt and white, cotton tank top. The desire to remove my ponytail as a way to hide more of myself was a nagging urge.

I let my mind take me somewhere else for the rest of the ride. I felt like an empty shell sitting there until the sound of his voice brought me back to reality. "Jess, let's go!"

We stopped at a gas station for sodas. I hopped out of the truck, and we walked inside together. My father and I would never talk about this again.

Chapter 5

Over the next few months, things only became worse. Somehow Mom and Dad managed to keep their jobs at the gas station, but barely. My mother's drinking was out of control, and I was losing count of how many times a week she threatened to kill herself. She told Paul and I that we would have a better life if she died. She didn't seem to know anything about what was best for us, and it bothered me that she pretended she did. Paul and I were blamed for the fighting and why she and Dad argued so much. Mom said if we weren't such pain in the asses, she and Dad wouldn't be so stressed all the time.

One evening, after hearing Mom and Dad yelling at each other in their bedroom, I came inside the trailer to see what was going on, mostly to make sure Mom wasn't hurting herself. Mom looked over at me as I walked in.

"Jess! Tell your dad how badly he treats me sometimes. He won't listen to me anymore," she said as she threw her hands into the air.

I hesitated.

"I don't want to get in the middle," I said timidly.

"Oh, fine. Ya know what? To hell with you too!"

"Wow, Lureen. You're too much," Dad responded. "I'm gettin' outta here."

He grabbed his keys, and after struggling for a moment to get away, he made it down the hall and was out the door. I followed behind him, asking if I could go with him. This wasn't something I usually did, but I knew she was mad at me and I didn't want to be left alone with her. He told me I had to stay, and within seconds, his truck started up, and his tires skid out of the driveway.

As soon as he was gone, my mother got a rope and tied me to a chair in the middle of the yard. She tied my hands behind my back and bound my feet together. She left me there and went back inside the trailer, but when my crying got too loud, she rushed back outside with duct tape and sealed my mouth shut. I sat there tied up until the sun went down. I eventually wet myself from not being able to use the bathroom.

Two days later, a woman in a white sedan pulled up in front of our trailer. Paul and I whispered to one another as we secretly watched her from the window. She was dressed in a gray skirt and jacket, and she held a binder in her left arm. I sprung off the couch and ran back to Mom's room to tell her we had a visitor.

The woman was from Child Protective Services. Mom had warned us one day this might happen. Neighbors had threatened her and Dad once before that they were going to call CPS if they heard us screaming. That's why she always told us to shut up. After the threat, my mother told us what to do if it ever happened.

"Lie," she said. "If they ask if we've ever hit you, you laugh at them! Tell them never! Got it?" Paul and I nodded our heads in agreement.

The woman knocked on the door, and with a sweet smile and soft tone, my mother answered the door.

"Hi, Mrs. Jennings. Child Protective Services received a call from someone concerned about your children. May I speak to you?"

My mother stepped outside while Paul and I waited anxiously on the couch. After speaking for a moment, Mom opened the front door.

"Hi, Jessica. May I speak to you for a minute?" the woman asked as she peeked her head inside.

Mom stepped inside the trailer, and the woman and I took a seat on the plastic chairs in the front yard. After introducing herself, she began her questions.

"Have your mommy and daddy ever put their hands on you?"

"No way," I said. In my mind, I thought of how they both did, in very different ways.

"Okay. Have they ever *accidentally* hurt you?"

"No, never," I said.

After several more minutes, she called Paul outside and asked the same series of questions. She then walked through the trailer briefly, then left. The woman never came back.

School, which I had once loved, was now a place where I meandered through the day worrying about what violent brawl was taking place at home. I worried that, if left alone for too long, my parents would kill each other.

Paul had a normal, loving relationship with our father, and sometimes he seemed to be the better liked child by our mother, but he still dealt with a great deal of dysfunction and abuse himself. He too saw Mom's drunkenness, and he heard the screaming and suicide threats. I knew he felt fear and stress, too. So I tried to protect him from these things in the little ways I could, and I stayed calm when we were together in stressful situations. I thought that if he saw me unbothered and unemotional, then he would be less likely to become scared or upset.

But there were days that we got the brunt of Mom's temper no matter what we did or how well we behaved. One day after Mom had been drinking, she got up and came down the hall screaming at Paul and me for being too noisy in the living room.

Paul talked back to her so she slapped him all over his arms and legs. When he began to scream, she held her hand over his mouth and whispered to him to shut up. This only made him scream louder because not being able to breathe out of his mouth scared him. He shook his head back and forth, trying to get her to uncover his mouth, but Mom became even angrier and continued to slap him.

Finally, he stopped screaming enough that she let go of him. By the time that happened, Paul's face was covered in red welts and scratches.

"And you too!" she said to me. Her voice was low and gravely from crying and drinking all day.

She grabbed my face and pressed her fingers into my cheeks. She held me there against the couch and pressed her fingers harder until I could feel her fingernails digging into my skin.

"Stop!" I began to cry.

"What're you cryin' about? I'll give you a reason to cry!"

She pressed her fingers harder into my cheeks, then she held my head backward and slapped the side of my face. The harder she hit, the harder I cried. This made her angrier. She leaned in close and looked at me; I could feel her breath on my face.

"Shut your mouth," she said in a low, angry whisper.

She placed her hand over my mouth to stop me from making noise, and she used her other hand to grab a chunk of my hair. She held me there until I became quiet, which I did quickly. Then she let go and went back to her room, flinging her door shut behind her.

While sitting on the couch with our hair messy and faces red, there was no better way for Paul and me to feel some satisfaction than for us to throw our middle fingers in the air toward Mom's closed door and make faces at her. I watched Paul as he stood up, wiggle both middle fingers in the air, and do a little dance. We covered our mouths to muzzle our laughter, but Paul wasn't done. Standing up, he paused and looked at Mom's bedroom door, then back at me. Then, he turned around, pulled down his pants, and shook his naked butt at her. We erupted in laughter, and Paul quickly pulled up his jeans and sat back down. We crossed our hands, put them on our lap, and then giggled until we no longer felt the stinging or welts on our skin.

Paul and I soon developed new coping mechanisms and ways to protect ourselves from the harsh treatment at home. I tried first by never giving my mother a reason to be mad at me. But when that didn't work, I stopped caring. Soon I realized when my mother told me that she hated me or when she blamed me for being the reason she wanted to die, it didn't provoke even the slightest emotion within me.

And even though Mom wasn't affectionate, she was very emotional. She became upset and cried often. Eventually, I was the opposite; it became impossible for me to cry about anything. However, the lack of reaction from me caused Mom to get even angrier. "You evil snake," she'd say. Or she would shout profanities at me and then call me cold hearted when I didn't react to it. But Mom didn't realize that between her and Dad, they had made me that way.

Paul had other ways of dealing with things. Now when he got hit by Mom and Dad, he'd laugh at them once they were all done. With his blue eyes red from crying and his blonde hair matted from putting up a fight, he'd tell them that the leather belt didn't hurt him and that they weren't even any good at spanking. He'd then run off outside and make them catch him if they wanted to spank him again. It took real guts for him to do that, and I always laughed and admired him for it.

As I got a little older, I accepted the relationship I had with my mother. I knew that underneath all the alcohol and drugs, my mother was a good person. I didn't have resentment or bitterness toward her, and anger was too heavy of a burden to carry. I still loved her, and somehow, even at a young age, I understood that my mother was broken inside.

I knew that life had not been kind to my mother, and it made her the way she was. She told me stories about when she was young and how life at home was troublesome for her and her six siblings. By the time my mother was eleven years old, she was sneaking alcohol from her mother's cabinet to cope with her emotions. Not long after that, she began smoking cigarettes. Then, by her teenage years, she was experimenting with an array of hallucinogenic and dissociative drugs. She told me that life at school wasn't any easier. She once shared a story of when she was in junior high, a boy walked up to her in the hallway and placed a brown paper bag over her head. With a crowd of people standing near him, he told her that she was hideous and that she should hide herself so others didn't have to see her. I could never understand why someone would do this to her.

After seeing my father hide his lies so well, it became harder for me to know whom to trust. I couldn't help but secretly question people's motives behind everything they did and wonder what kind of person they really were when no one else was around. I was eager to understand why people were the way they were and what made them do the things they did.

I struggled with how I was supposed to view my father. He did his best to provide for us, and he didn't hit me and Paul half as much as our mother did. In fact, he felt sorry for us when she did. Even he was hit by her when she was angry. I would watch her swing at him repeatedly, and he would never raise a fist to her. I guess after all of my mother's stories about men beating her, I admired this about him. I wrestled with these feelings, causing me to never really know if I loved my father or not.

Chapter 6

Right before fifth grade started, Dad's dad, Grandpa Ray, passed away. Paul and I had never met him or even spoken to him on the phone. Most of Dad's family lived 3,000 miles away in upstate New York so there were a lot of relatives we'd never met. But, after not seeing any of them for over a decade, Dad was determined to take the trip there to properly say goodbye to his father.

As soon as he heard the news, Dad called his boss, Roger. Roger owned the gas station, and he had a soft spot for Mom, Dad, Paul, and me. When Mom and Dad somehow got stuck working the same shifts, Roger would let me and Paul hang out at the gas station and have candy. He also gave Mom and Dad as many shifts as he could, knowing that they always needed the extra money. So when Dad asked Roger about taking time off to go to New York, he not only agreed but gave Mom the time off too. He said it was a trip the whole family should take together. Of course, living the way we did and with multiple addictions to pay for, my parents didn't have the money for four plane tickets. Roger offered to pay for all four tickets and said Mom and Dad could work overtime to pay them off. We couldn't believe it.

I had always dreamed of getting on an airplane to go somewhere, and even though we were going for my grandpa's funeral, I couldn't help but be just a little excited to see someplace new. Before this, we had never been further than two hours away from home.

A few days passed, and we were packing our bags for the following morning's flight. Somehow this distraction made it feel almost like we were a family again. We were all getting along, and it felt like all of our problems were on pause just for a brief moment.

The flight was long, but I was too excited to sleep. I kept busy by staring out at the clouds and reading a book that I had checked out from the library the day before. By the time we landed and were driven to Grandpa's house, it was 1:00 a.m. The next seven days we spent running around our grandmother's ranch, playing with cousins, swimming, feeding the pigs in the barn, and riding three wheelers. The go-kart was off limits after day two when I drove it in underneath a car because the brakes didn't work and I had no way to stop it. I slid under the car while the muffler shaved off layers of skin from my knee down to my shin, leaving me in wrapped in layers of bandages the rest of the trip.

With our rental car, we wandered the backcountry of New York. We even drove up to the Canadian border to spend a day in Canada. However, once we got there, we were told we weren't allowed in because of Mom's criminal record. Mom and Dad shouted profanities out the window and flipped off the Border Patrol as we drove away while Paul and I laughed from the backseat. We were low class, and I knew it, but I didn't care. We were together and happy. Plus, Mom and Dad hadn't argued once on the trip. I enjoyed the kind of family we were while we were there. Something about New York was magical, and it was nothing like our life in California.

It turned out that Mom and Dad felt the same way. At the end of our trip, as we loaded up our luggage into the car and said goodbye to everyone, I heard Mom and Dad telling the family that they were considering starting over in New York. This surprised me since they hadn't even mentioned it to Paul and me. But, as I sat in the backseat thinking about it, I began to like the idea.

Within days of arriving back in California, it was official: Mom and Dad decided we were moving. They told Paul and me that they felt it would be good for us. It was an opportunity for us to start fresh in a place where we had the support of a large family.

I was torn; I wanted to be a happy family like we were in New York, but I had a lot of worries. I felt that once the excitement of the move was over, the fighting would begin again, along with the drinking and the threats from my mother that she would kill herself. We simply would've just packed up all of our problems and brought them to New York. And I couldn't shake the thought of my mother drinking and driving along the dark, rural roads of upstate New York. Also, the thought of moving started to feel more like a life sentence of keeping these secrets about my father. If I was going to tell my mother, or anyone, about what my father was doing, it would've had to be before, not after, we made the move 3,000 miles away. My mother wouldn't have any family or friends out there of her own. If I didn't speak up now, then I would lose my opportunity.

Everything began to change quickly, and within a few short weeks, my parents had purchased an old moving truck to get us across the country. My father, shirtless and greasy, drove up to the trailer to showcase the new moving truck, which was rather comical, considering that it was certainly nothing to showcase. It was old; dirty; and from the way the transmission was grinding when he shifted, it didn't sound reliable. This thing was supposed to make it from California to New York, and I had no idea how that would be possible. Later that day, I found Dad under the hood, trying to get our new moving truck to start back up.

Next, my parents notified our teachers. Mrs. Lucas, my fifth grade teacher, arranged a class party for me as a way for everyone to say goodbye. At first, I felt elated that there would be a party in *my* honor. But I was still skeptical that we would actually make it out of California. My mother and father were unreliable; it was hard for me to believe this move would happen. The thought of having a goodbye party and then facing my classmates and telling everyone that I wasn't moving after all was dreadful. However, just a couple weeks later, the party happened. I walked into the classroom on my last day and saw the large banner hanging with handwritten notes from all the students. I felt loved and suddenly optimistic. It seemed it was all going to happen after all.

Paul and I were officially taken out of school, and before the weekend was over, our little trailer that I had spent my life living in was sold. The next day, we'd start our journey across the country.

Three days had gone by, and we still hadn't left California. Actually, we hadn't even left town, and we had spent the last two nights sleeping in the back of our Toyota pickup truck. Things didn't pan out the way they were supposed to, and Dad said we needed to stay in California for a few more days. Turns out the old moving truck we purchased, which was now full of all our belongings, had broken down and needed major repairs. Disappointed, my brother and I did the only thing we could do: shut up and wait.

Three days turned into a week, and before we knew it, we were no longer sleeping under the camper shell of our dad's Toyota, but we were now sleeping in an old 10x10 storage unit. The unit belonged to a new friend my parents had made, and despite not having a shower, a toilet, or even a bed, it was what we had now.

The storage unit was cold, dirty, and full of what looked to me like useless junk. Tattered cardboard boxes lined the cement floor while old car parts were placed in small piles in-between them. An old dusty lamp propped up on a tower of boxes was connected to a long orange extension cord to give us light. We pushed crates and boxes aside and cleared an area in the center to make a small bed. We took the blankets we had and stacked them until we could no longer feel the cold cement underneath our bodies. With our coats and shoes on, we lay on the floor at night, trying to fall asleep. The repeated flick of the lighter, and the deep coughing right outside the metal roll up door let us know that our parents weren't very far.

I grew impatient as the days went on. And because the plan was for us to still move, my brother and I were not in school. We were dragged along with Mom and Dad all day long. I didn't know it was possible because I was so used to their behavior, but I was disappointed in them. But I was also mad at myself. I was mad that I thought they might actually follow through with the move, and I was mad that I let myself become excited for it.

After a few more nights living in the storage unit, while the metal door was partially rolled up, Mom and Dad were spotted by security. A man in a golf cart rode by while patrolling the property, and we were told that we needed to leave the following day. With nowhere else to go, Paul and I slept in the truck while our parents stayed up all night. They never slept these days. In fact, I couldn't remember the last time I saw either of them sleeping. And the friends they were spending time with were the same way; not only did they not sleep, but they didn't even have a place to go home to. I truly began to appreciate all we had before living this way.

By the third week of homelessness, it was more apparent than ever that New York was a dream long gone. My parents had stopped talking about the move and were completely immersed in their new lifestyle of drugs and homelessness while Paul and I had no choice but to join them for the ride. After several more weeks, Paul and I were put back into school. My worst nightmare had come true. I was going to have to explain to everyone why my family didn't move. The thought of my first day back filled me with dread. I was so embarrassed I came up with a lie to tell anyone who asked me why I came back. I told them my father was offered a job in California that paid so well he couldn't possibly have turned it down.

Shortly after starting school again, our parents acquired a small camper for us to live in. At about eight feet long, it was smaller than what we were used to, but I was grateful for it. It was a roof over our heads, and it even had a real bed. We would have to figure out where we would find showers, but so far, we were off to a good start. And within a few days, my parents came up with an idea: we'd go camping. Or at least we'd be calling it that.

The four of us drove up the long winding road to Anthony Chabot Campgrounds in Castro Valley. If we were able to stay there, then we wouldn't have to worry about parking the camper on the street, and we would have access to water and electricity.

Nervous, yet hopeful, I watched the twists and turns of the road that would lead the way to a temporary home, and about thirty minutes later, we arrived.

My father put the truck in park and hopped out to have a word with the park attendant while the three of us waited anxiously inside the truck for his return. Just moments later, he swung open the driver side door, and with a large grin on his face, he said, "We're in!"

We all sighed with relief, and I immediately felt the mood lighten. To anyone else, this may have seemed insignificant and even silly, but not to me. This was good news for us; we had spent the past few weeks without a place to live, and even once we got the camper, we had no safe place to park. We wouldn't have to worry about any of that for a few days.

We made our way down the small winding turns toward our campsite. It felt like a treasure hunt as Mom directed Dad on how to get there.

The first day was unforgettable. Tall, fragrant, eucalyptus trees surrounded us. Birds of all sorts chirped in the tops of the trees as the sun peeked through the gray branches. Blue Jays hopped across the leaves that blanketed our camp site. It was enchanting, like something out of a movie. And there wasn't a car horn or siren to be heard anywhere near us. There was stillness and peace here, and I was perfectly content with where I was.

Chapter 7

Right before our three day stay at Anthony Chabot was thought to be over, Dad spoke to the attendant and was able to get permission from the park to continue our stay for an additional two and a half months. There was a park rule that said that the same person cannot camp for more than ninety days out of the year. The attendant agreed to allow us to use all ninety days consecutively, which gave us about two months and four weeks more. I was ecstatic!

However, there were some things about this new living arrangement which I learned I didn't like, such as knowing mountain lions roamed the hills, the sounds that came after dark, or having to walk to the restroom by myself with a flashlight. But I still felt living here was much better than living in an old storage unit or the back of Dad's pickup truck or having to park our camper on dark side streets while we slept at night. I was thankful. I would put up with the scary walks to the bathroom as long as we could stay.

Because the drive from Anthony Chabot was so long and we didn't always have the gas, there were many days my brother and I didn't go to school. The drive there was about thirty minutes, not including the time it took to stop to drop Paul off at his school on the way. If we were lucky, we would arrive on time, and if we didn't, then I wished I had just stayed home. I hated being late and watching the other students stare as I walked into the classroom. And on the days that both my brother and I *would* make it to school, there was no telling if, or when, we'd get picked up. There were plenty of days I sat on the curb—sometimes for two hours, sometimes up to three—waiting for someone to come get me. I'd watch the kids one by one getting into their cars or walking home until I was the only one left. Of course, Paul was also waiting, just like I was, at his school.

After a couple more weeks, some excitement of the campground wore off, but I was still happy there. I loved knowing where I was sleeping at night, and stability had become a very valuable thing to me. I still enjoyed the nature all around us. I loved spotting deer and watching the birds flutter through the trees. And I loved sitting around the campfire at night while hearing the crackling of the wood.

Soon, my mother began to sleep again at night. It was a nice change to see her quietly sleeping in bed. She looked peaceful and calm. However, she wasn't just sleeping at night but during the day also. When I'd arrive back after school, I would find her still asleep in the small bed of the camper.

Suddenly, this became the new normal, and it was rare to find her awake doing anything, even eating or using the bathroom. Mom would only wake up enough to just barely open her eyes as Paul and I stood in front of her, offering her food. She'd open her eyes just slightly to clumsily shove a piece of food into her mouth, then fall back asleep.

Days would go by without us saying a word to her, even though she was just a few feet away. After a couple weeks of this, I learned from my father why she was sleeping so much. My mother had a new addiction: morphine. It made her absent in a whole new way. She was there physically, but not mentally, and honestly, I couldn't tell which version of my mother I preferred.

Within the coming weeks Mom's morphine supply was depleted and she was back to staying up all night with dad.

In an attempt for my father to bring some fun and excitement to our lives, he decided to use the large empty campground as a space to teach me how to drive. One morning, as he and I drove back from the showers, he casually offered to let me drive back. Without any hesitation and with pure joy, I shouted, "Yes!"

He smiled and pulled the car over to the side.

"You'll have to sit on my lap the first couple of times until you get the hang of it," he said as he patted his right thigh.

Suddenly, all of the excitement I had was gone, and instead, I felt deflated. I was uneasy. I wouldn't be just sitting on my father's lap; I'd be sitting on *his* lap. I struggled for a moment on what I should do, and I had a sense of shame if I were to go along with it. But, ultimately, I did. I was eleven years old and wanted nothing more than to learn to drive. I took the leap into the driver's seat and wrapped my hands tightly around the steering wheel. I slowly pressed my foot on the gas pedal and we took off.

Grinning ear to ear, I made my way over the small rolling hills leading to our campsite.

"This is easy!" I shouted.

"Well, you're a natural," he replied with a laugh. And I was convinced he was right.

Our ninety days were up, and this time, my father didn't have any tricks to extend our stay. There was nowhere else for us to go, and with both parents unemployed, there was no money. We were back to parking the camper out on the streets at night.

The past couple months we had survived by Mom and Dad recycling old scrap metal they were finding behind businesses or inside buildings. This became the only way they would make money. Sometimes it was old parts thrown in the dumpster, or other times it was machinery that they could disassemble and recycle. The small amounts of cash they got by doing this allowed my brother and me to eat every day. It also allowed my parents to maintain their methamphetamine, pot, and alcohol addictions as well as keep small amounts of gas in the car, just enough to get us where we were going but not enough to keep us from running out on the way home.

Soon Mom and Dad were dumpster diving and hoarding almost everything they could get their hands on. Our days and nights now consisted of driving through industrial areas until they spotted a business that had something that appeared valuable. I hated this more than anything else, and Mom and Dad told me I was stuck up for not enjoying it as much as they did.

Paul and I were told to stay in the car while they scoped out the premises and disappeared for long periods of time. It could be twenty minutes or two hours; we never knew. This often led to neglected schoolwork and a lack of sleep because we didn't get to bed until late. Paul and I rode along with them for hours while they got in and out of the car repeatedly to look inside every large dumpster they came across.

To make matters more frustrating, most of the items they pulled out of the trash to take home with us were complete garbage, like an old chipped paperweight or old worn out pair of shoes. It was no wonder they were thrown away in the first place.

But, as frustrating as it all was, I didn't say a word. I kept quiet and stayed out of trouble. My brother and I just sat in the car and talked to each other while we were told to be on the lookout. We were told to make a loud sound or honk the horn if we saw any cop cars pulling up.

Paul and I had gotten quite used to encountering the police. We were always getting pulled over for things like expired tags on the car, or sometimes we'd get pulled over for just looking suspicious. Maybe it was the vehicle we were in or the fact that they were driving around businesses late at night looking for things to steal. The cops were hard-nosed with Mom and Dad but always kind to Paul and me. One night, while we were pulled over, one of the officers had the two of us stand against the warm headlights of his patrol car while he cracked jokes and made friendly conversation with us. The other police officers searched our car and then lectured Mom and Dad for having us out so late at night.

But even then, Paul and I knew to never tell the cops the truth about what our parents were doing.

There were times after hours of driving around in the dark, hungry and thirsty, that I felt I couldn't take it anymore. But I knew better than to raise my voice to my parents. That would undoubtedly get me a beating from my mother. If I said anything to set her off, not only would I get hit, but there was a good chance it would provoke an argument between her and Dad. I was conditioned to work through all of my feelings and problems in my own head. It was the only thing I could safely do that didn't upset or provoke anyone else.

Soon the cash Mom and Dad were making proved to not be enough for them, and they needed a way to make more money. They began siphoning gas from strangers' cars and stealing tags off of people's license plates so we wouldn't have to pay for registration. If my parents could find metal piping, especially anything made of copper, which was the most lucrative, they would find a way to get it.

I remember my father telling us about a new way he found to make a lot of money quickly. He was going to recycle catalytic convertors, a part underneath vehicles. It only posed one small difficulty: you only found them while still attached to a perfectly running car. This proved to be only a minor inconvenience for him.

He had a tool bag ready with everything he needed to be able to remove them from cars as quickly as he could. I felt bad for the poor unsuspecting victims who were now missing a piece of their car.

The three of us would wait in the truck as Dad went into the office to get cash for his metal. We'd watch him walk back out to the truck and flash us the wad of cash he had just made. It was exciting at first until we realized once again that most of the money wouldn't go toward things we needed, but to drugs and alcohol.

Paul and I became used to the constant feeling of hunger, but some days were harder than others. We went to school each day on an empty stomach and having to spend 12:15-1:00 p.m. watching the other students eat was tough. At some schools they offered free or discounted lunches, but for some reason, which I can't remember, we didn't get them. Daily lunches were $2.25, and I seldom was given the money to buy one. Each day at lunch time, I'd sit at the same concrete bench with my friends and pretend that I didn't buy lunch because I wasn't hungry. Occasionally, a friend would offer her leftovers to me, and I'd say no thank you and insist that I wasn't hungry. It pained me to turn down food, but I didn't want anyone finding out the truth about how hungry I actually was and that I couldn't afford the lunches. Only when a friend was insistent about me eating did I give in, but not without first pretending to be annoyed by their persistence. I'm not sure I fooled anyone, but I had to try. I suppose all I had left was my pride, and I was doing all I could to hold on to what was left of it.

After parking the camper on the streets for several weeks, my parents made an agreement with a man who owned a local catering truck yard and warehouse. My parents would provide security to the yard that housed the fifty trucks at night, and in exchange, they would allow us to park our camper in the back corner of the yard without paying any rent. Essentially, my parents were hired to protect the yard from drug-addicted criminals just like themselves. Ideally, this arrangement should've worked perfectly for everyone involved. Since neither of my parents needed sleep because of the continuous supply of methamphetamine they smoked each day, this would allow them to be up during the late hours of the night, providing the security they promised, and their extreme paranoia and fixation on sounds would be an added layer of security not offered by other *normal* people.

In exchange, my brother and I gained some stability since we knew where we'd be coming home to each night. And the promise of eventually being able to hook up to the business's electricity source so we could have power and even watch television was exciting. Or having light to be able to read at night. Or do anything at night for that matter. It was the small things I had come to appreciate so much.

As we settled into our new living arrangement, Dad's visits began again after a brief hiatus while we lived at the campground. Soon after moving into the yard, Mom and Dad acquired a trailer, which they would sleep in while Paul and I continued to sleep in the camper. I remember the disappointment I felt that early morning as I felt Dad pulling my covers off me. I suppose I had started to hope that these things weren't going to happen anymore.

Soon, living at the yard became normal to me, although I knew other people didn't live this way. The disapproving looks given from the food truck workers reminded me that our family was really just an uncivilized embarrassment. I was ashamed of myself for having been excited about living in an old yard or having electricity. Seeing people look at me this way made me feel low, and I dreamt of the day when I felt normal, like other people. When my family didn't drive a vehicle that had Mountain

Dew cans falling out of it when we opened the door, or when we could afford to buy something to eat other than cans of corned beef hash from the dollar store.

Living there didn't last long though, and within a few months, we were told it was time for us to go. I wondered what the reason was for the sudden eviction, but I had some ideas. Because of heavy drug use, my parents argued with each other a lot. There were loud, violent spectacles that occurred several times a week. When Mom was upset, she had no sense of shame, and all reason went out the window. Many times, I stood by mortified as I watched her scream profanities at my father while countless workers stood by to watch. The looks on their faces were a mixture of amusement and shock. I didn't blame them for their discreet side whispers to one another. I would've stared too; it was hard not to.

I felt relieved whenever these arguments happened after dark because there usually wasn't anyone else around to witness them. Like the night Paul and I stood together and watched Mom and Dad scream at one another until finally our mother abruptly stopped yelling and quickly made her way to the trailer. She stepped inside, and seconds later, the door flung wide open as she came out and charged toward the car. Paul and I stood by watching her, wondering what she'd do next.

"I can't take this anymore!" she screamed. She jumped in the driver's seat and started up the car.

"What're you gonna do now, huh!" Dad shouted back while throwing his hands up in the air.

My mother had been drinking heavily that day so she knew she'd get a reaction from us by doing this. Much calmer than our father, Paul and I stood about ten feet away before we slowly began to approach the car.

"Mom, don't go," I said softly, hoping to reason with her.

"Yeah, stay here, Mom," Paul told her while holding back his tears.

Without responding to either of us, she continued yelling at our father. Paul and I stepped away and stood by to watch. Mom then pressed her foot onto the gas pedal while simultaneously holding down the brake with her other foot. The tires screeched loudly, and smoke began to cloud around the car while they continued to scream and curse at one another.

Then suddenly, Mom took her foot off the brake and plowed her car straight into the cement building several yards in front of her. We heard the metal smash against the building and the yellow plastic from the headlights shatter and fall to the ground.

Paul and I rushed over to the car as Dad turned and walked away. Her body was hunched over, and her head rested on the steering wheel. Her eyes were closed, but she was breathing and didn't appear to be bleeding. We gently shook her and called her name, but she didn't respond. We stood near the driver side door and waited to see movement from her, and after calling her name several more times, we gave up and walked away. I sensed that she could hear us calling her name, but it wasn't the attention from my brother and me that she wanted—it was our father's.

Shortly after this, there was a day that was by far the most embarrassing, and when I thought I had seen it all, I hadn't. One late afternoon while lines of food trucks were making their way into the yard, an argument began between Mom and Dad. My mother was accusing him of taking her for granted and not giving her the credit she deserved for helping to provide for the family. The yard was full of people parking their trucks to clean and prepare for the next day. While my mother had the largest audience she could ask for, she made herself *known* to everyone. Wearing nothing more than a small satin robe, untied, she barreled out of the trailer door after our father. The entire front of my mother's body was exposed to everyone as she screamed profanities at the top of her lungs. I looked around to see the people stopped, looking at us.

Embarrassed, my father walked away from her, hoping she would leave him alone and go back inside. Instead, my mother began running toward him. I looked at her, then I looked back at the people watching. I was mortified.

My father turned around to her, and in a low, angry voice, he demanded that she get back in the house. "Everyone can see you," he said, slowly enunciating every word. He then turned his back toward her and continued walking away.

"It's so easy for you to leave, isn't it, Todd?!" Mom shouted.

She ran after him again and then begged him not to leave. He walked faster toward the truck, but before he could get there, she reached for him by grabbing the back of his shirt. He tried to fling her off of him, but she held on tighter.

Then, in front of everyone, she fell to the ground. "Don't leave me right now. I need you," she begged, being dragged as Dad walked.

"Lureen, get off of me." He was so angry that his teeth were clenched as he spoke.

Still, she held on to him as he struggled to get away from her. The next thing I knew, my mother's robe slipped off of her, and her naked body was dragged along the grimy asphalt. The crowd stared, and no one made a sound. Horrified, I retreated into the trailer.

Perhaps these were the reasons we were told we had to leave.

Chapter 8

Directly on the other side of the catering yard was a large gravel yard used to store vehicles. My father had recently met with the man who owned the yard, offering him the same security services he had provided the catering yard. So before we were moved onto the street, we were moving our things just about twenty yards away to the other side of the fence.

    I felt indifferent about the move, although I did feel relieved that I wouldn't have to face the people that watched the brawl between my parents. But this new yard was much darker and had a creepy feeling at night. Perhaps because of the cars and trucks covered in cobwebs and surrounded by overgrown weeds. However, on the opposite side of the yard, there was a fence that we shared with the police department. This should have made me feel safer, but it didn't. In fact, it made me nervous because of the row of marijuana plants my parents were now growing. They threw black tarps over our side of the fence and told us to say they were tomato plants if anyone ever asked. But the plants grew taller and taller, and no one ever said a word about it.

    One night, after spending the day with our friends who lived in the neighborhood on the other side of the alley, Paul and I called it a night and headed home. At the back corner of the development, there was a fence with a hole in it. We crawled through that, walked down the alley, and then crawled through a hole in another fence which led to the yard we lived in.

When Paul and I arrived back, we were surprised to see that there was a large box full of food on the table. We were elated. We weren't used to seeing that much food at one time. We never had groceries at home, and even if we did, we didn't have running water or electricity so we weren't able to cook anything.

The box was full of random items like crackers, muffins, juices, and candy bars. I would've loved things like bread, lunch meat, or milk, but I was grateful to have what my parents had bought for us. As Paul and I scrounged through the box in excitement, Mom and Dad stood by, watching us with grins on their faces.

"So where did you guys buy all this stuff?" I asked while tearing open the plastic wrapper of a banana muffin.

Paul stood opposite of me, gathering the snacks that he was claiming as his own.

"Well, ya won't believe it. There's this dumpster behind the ol' building we get metal from that has all this perfectly good food."

Mom's eyes were wide with excitement as she told us, and Dad laughed as she explained it. I couldn't help but feel let down while I tried to not let my face show it. Every so often, the reality that our family was nothing more than a low-class, destitute bunch slapped me in the face again. Mom and Dad surprised us with food they found in an old dumpster, and they expected us to be excited about it. What was worse was that we *were* excited about it. Mom and Dad had too much pride, they said, to take from the system by using food stamps or financial assistance, but this was not even a blip on their radar. I wondered if they could've tried just a little harder before resorting to this. It was like they had given up completely, but I suppose they had a long time ago. I threw my standards aside and indulged.

It didn't take long for this to become the way my brother and I would eat from that point forward. Mom and Dad didn't even consider buying food from the grocery store or even burgers from McDonald's when they could pick up "perfectly good" food that was free.

One day, in broad daylight, Mom and Dad were dumpster diving in the large metal dumpster behind Target. A woman drove by and looked at Paul and me as we sat in the backseat of the car while Mom and Dad's legs hung out of the dumpster. Seconds later, she turned her car around and came back. She parked, got out, and then walked up to our window.

"Are you two hungry?" she asked me as she peeked into the backseat.

Paul and I quickly responded with "yes," thinking she had food to give us. Instead, she walked up to Mom and Dad and handed them a twenty-dollar bill.

"Excuse me! Please take this. Buy your children some food," she said.

"Wow, thank you," Mom and Dad said to her.

The woman handed Mom the money and then walked away. She smiled at Paul and me as she walked past us and back to her car. Needless to say, Mom and Dad didn't buy food with the money that woman gave them.

Mom and Dad's evening drives around the local industrial areas continued. They spent hours each night stopping at every dumpster they saw, searching for anything they thought could be sold or recycled. Paul and I sat in the backseat as we watched them hop inside the trash bins with flashlights.

Once it got late and Paul was nodding off, I'd tap him on the shoulder to let him know he could lay his head down on my lap and sleep. He never hesitated to take me up on the offer, and he'd quickly drift off to sleep while I kept watch out the window. Paul was always quick to return the favor. When I was uncomfortable and suffering from another migraine, he'd always insist I laid my head on *his* lap and rest.

No matter what, Paul and I knew that we had each other. We fought and yelled at one another but we also laughed and had fun together. Like the time I convinced Paul that he was invisible. I had Mom and Dad both agree to go along with it and after ignoring him for nearly forty-five minutes Paul was convinced. He began to cry hysterically and jump around to try to get our attention. I felt so bad that I told him that his legs were suddenly starting to reappear and that we could see him again. The small moments of kindness and humor between us brought glimpses of humanity back into my life.

During one of these nightly drives, Mom and Dad came across a dumpster behind a bakery. When they got inside it, they found that it was filled with bags of animal cookies. The bright pink-and-white cookies dotted with colorful sprinkles. Of course, Mom and Dad loaded the back of the car with as many bags as they could grab. These cookies then became our breakfast and lunch, and after two weeks of eating them, I began to hate them. I vowed I would never eat another animal cookie again no matter how hungry I was.

I didn't have an easy time at school, and by the seventh grade, I had more insecurities than ever before. I wasn't anything like the other girls at school, and I didn't have the basic things that others had. At home, we didn't have running water or electricity; we didn't even have a working toilet.

But this also meant we didn't have a functioning washer and dryer either so we didn't have a way to wash our clothes. I tried hand-washing things using bottles of water, but even then, we still didn't have any laundry detergent or a way to dry them. There were times in the colder months that hanging my clothes to dry wasn't sufficient, and I'd walk to school in clothes that were still wet.

Living this way, I grew to appreciate everything, like being able to finally buy deodorant so the girls in the locker room wouldn't whisper about me or buying a disposable razor because unshaven underarms also didn't go unnoticed by middle school girls. I knew what it was like to go without the very essentials in a girl's life, like properly fitting clothes or tampons.

However, I decided to do something about that. Right before my twelfth birthday, I got my very first job and I began earning my own money for these things.

I was hired by a retired woman named Jackie who lived in the neighborhood on the other side of the fence. She could've been my grandmother's age. Many times she had driven by as I was hopping through the hole in the fence so I was pretty sure she knew where I lived.

One day, Jackie saw me while I was passing by her house and she called me over to her porch as she stood outside. It turned out that she wanted to hire me to clean her house for her one to two times a week. I couldn't have been happier, and I agreed to clean for her as much as she needed.

Jackie was kind to me, and she compensated me generously. Each shift I was paid $50 for two hours work. On days she needed extra dusting or the refrigerator cleaned, she'd pay up to $70. She even made me lunch after each shift, and every once in a while, she would even take me out to the deli down the road.

I enjoyed working for her, but I was terrified of her dog, Bane. Bane was vicious. From behind the flimsy baby gate, he'd snarl at me while I cleaned, and whenever I got too close to the gate while vacuuming, he'd lunge toward me. I feared that one day he'd knock over the gate and get to me. In spite of that, I returned every week. Nothing was going to get in my way of working.

With the money I made working for Jackie, I was able to buy some things I needed. After payday, I'd walk to the Walmart about half a mile up the road, and I'd eagerly make my way to the girls' section. I'd carefully look through the racks of cute shirts and accessories, and I'd take my time to make sure I spent my money on the best choice. After, I'd usually go to the boy's section to find Paul a shirt or something I knew he needed. I knew that he was in need of things just as much as I was, and I almost felt guilty that I had a job and he didn't.

After carefully picking out the things I was going to buy, I felt pleased with myself. Before I could even leave the store, I'd go into the restroom and change into my new clothes. I felt so good about myself as I walked home. I almost felt normal. I was used to standing out from the crowd because of the clothes I wore, the beat-up car my parents drove us in, or because of where we lived. And although I did everything I could to look like everyone else, I felt like they all knew I was different. But I had hope this would begin to change now. After my trip to Walmart, I walked around with a wad of leftover ones in my pocket, and I felt unstoppable. I had more money than my own parents did, and I didn't need anyone else to take care of me.

After working for Jackie for several months, I arrived at her house one day ready for my shift, but to my surprise, she was drunk. She looked like a mess, and when I knocked on the door, instead of her saying hello, she firmly told me to come in. The tone of her voice was angry, and it was apparent that she was upset. After she instructed me on the work she needed done that day, she went into her bedroom and shut the door.

Within an hour, I had completed her list and was ready to leave, although I was still hoping to be fed my usual lunch first. But this time, there was no lunch. Instead, Jackie came out of her room to speak to me before I left. Her eyes were red and puffy from crying.

"There's somethin' you need to know, and it's nobody else's business." Her words were slurred as she spoke.

"It's for your own good that you don't come over here when my husband is home."

I didn't know what this meant, and I wanted to ask questions, but I didn't. When I returned to work the following week, instead of answering the door, she yelled at me through the window and told me to leave and never come back. I never really knew what happened that day or why I lost my job.

Early one morning, about a week later, I woke up to the sound of a metal rake being pulled along the gravel outside while Mom had a conversation with a friend of hers. My mother raked the yard constantly. When she was especially strung out, it was something she fixated on. I was sure that every person that had ever come over had seen my mother with a rake in her hands. It became a joke, even to her.

It was overcast and chilly, but I decided to get up and go outside. I stepped out of the trailer, and I stared at my mother. She was cleaning the yard in the new blue jeans that I had just bought with the money I earned.

As I stood there, I began counting the grease stains that were now all over the front of them. They were ruined. I finally had a good pair of jeans to wear to school, and they were destroyed. I stood there speechless. But that wasn't all. As I looked at her, I noticed that she was also wearing my shoes—a black pair of Nikes I had just bought from a secondhand store. They were caked with mud.

My blood boiled. I couldn't stand to even look at my mother, but I didn't say anything. On the rare occasion that I got upset with her, it inevitably led to her starting a fight with Dad or threatening to kill herself.

"If I'm such a bad mother, I should just kill myself shouldn't I?" she'd say.

Then sometimes she'd grab something sharp, like a knife, and hold it to her throat.

"You want me to do this, don't ya?" she'd say while clenching her teeth. "You ungrateful brat, you deserve to watch me die."

I never understood why my brother and I were the objects of her anger. We respected her and loved her.

Late one night, I lay in my bed, trying to fall asleep. The trailer was dark except for a light off in the distance, peeking through the small window above my bed.

I could hear my mother screaming from the other end of the yard as she argued with my father. I rolled over to my side, trying to ignore the noise and fall asleep. Suddenly, the window above my bed shattered, and an empty Heineken bottle flew over my head. It hit the other side of the wall, then bounced off, and landed at the foot of my bed. I quickly sat up and scooched backward until my back was against the wall. I was worried there may be another one coming. Glass shards now rested on top of my pillow. For a moment, I remained still, contemplating if it were worth my effort to get up and try to help diffuse the situation.

"You never loved me!" Mom shouted as she cried.

"You are crazy lady. You need help!" Dad said back to her.

"Ya know what, Todd? You're a real piece of work!"

I peeked out of the broken window and watched as Mom suddenly began to charge toward Dad. Exhausted, I let out a long sigh, then stood up. I stepped out of the trailer and felt the cold chill on my face. Immediately, I regretted getting up.

What I hadn't known while I was lying in bed was that Mom had poured a gallon of kerosene over her head. I stepped outside to find her blonde hair soaked with the highly flammable oil. She held out a lighter in her left hand and screamed at Dad, warning him she would light herself on fire if he came any closer to her.

Her bangs stuck tightly to her forehead while the longer pieces stuck to the sides of her face. Her mascara and eyeliner had formed dark circles under her eyes, and as I looked closer, I could see that the kerosene had run down her leather jacket and chest and soaked her jeans. She was drenched from head to toe.

"Don't come any closer! I'll light it, I swear to God!" she threatened.

I didn't know what to say. Mom rocked herself back and forth while holding out her lighter and screaming profanities at my father and her voice cracked from her incessant yelling. I stood by and quietly watched the uncontrollable mess my mother had become. I remained still and tried not to provoke her to flick the lighter she was holding.

"Do it! Just do it already!" Dad yelled at her.

I prayed that she wouldn't. My father only said things like that once he was past his breaking point, after she had exhausted him. My mother relished the reactions she got from all of us with her threats, and once my father stopped caring or reacting, it enraged her. She became an even more evil version of herself, and the tone of her voice deepened as if her demons were speaking for her. This was when I became frightened.

The standoff between the three of us continued for several more minutes until my father submitted to her and gave her what she wanted.

"I'm so sorry. I love you," he said as he embraced her.

Her yelling stopped, and she embraced him back. She and Dad held each other and whispered their apologies to one another. Exhausted, I walked back to the trailer, cleaned the glass off of my pillow, and attempted to go back to sleep.

Within a couple days, my mother would be back on suicide watch, which was usually my job several times a week. I'd help mediate the arguments between her and my father and help make sure that she didn't hurt herself too badly. Often I'd look around the house and gather anything sharp.

With my mother regularly threatening suicide, I was always worried that one day she'd successfully take her own life. So, I tried to keep her happy and cushion her from unnecessary stress because I feared that it just might be the thing that broke her. The stress of this left me in a never-ending cycle of stomach pain and headaches. And the anxiety was almost too much for me to bear. I needed someone to save me, but I was the one responsible for the saving. I couldn't seek help from Mom and Dad because I was the help.

Chapter 9

It was raining and there were leaks above my bed. I kept my face covered, trying to warm my nose. The window above my head had been repaired with duct tape and an old piece of cardboard, but the cold air still seeped in. And soon I felt the rain soaking through my blanket. I began to hear the *plop* of each raindrop as it fell into the puddles that had formed on my covers. I repositioned myself, trying to get comfortable without getting wetter. Then, as I lay there, I began to hear my mother crying outside.

I stepped outside and saw my mother sitting on the gravel, leaning up against a forklift that was being stored in our yard. I approached her quietly. Her hair was soaked with dark red blood that poured from her head, and she sat with her head back and eyes closed. She had just finished banging her head repeatedly against the solid metal forklift. She sat there quietly crying to herself because my father was nowhere to be found. I knelt down next to her so she knew she wasn't alone. Then I whispered, "Mom."

She let out a small noise.

"Are you okay?"

"I don't know, Jess," she whispered as her eyes stayed closed.

"Mom, let me help you get up. I can get you into bed," I said softly.

Her eyes opened slightly before rolling to the back of her head.

"Mom, let's get you in bed, okay?" I gently grasped her arm and helped her stand.

Together we walked into the trailer, I got her a towel and helped clean her up before getting her into bed.

One week later, I woke to my thirteenth birthday. I didn't expect much because we didn't have much, but I was excited to be a teenager.

"Mornin', Jess. Happy birthday, darlin'," Mom said as I stepped out of the trailer.

"Good morning, Mom."

"We'll find a way to get you some pizza or somethin' tonight, okay? Possibly fetch you a duck." Mom smiled. The year before, on Mom's birthday, I told her I had a gift for her and that I'd be back in one hour. I got on my bike and rode about two miles to a police station where there was a large man-made pond. Mom may have been hard on Paul and me, but she did have a soft side, especially for animals. With a piece of bread I had shoved in my pocket, I lured a duck over to me, and once it was close enough, I grabbed it. I then placed it inside a box that I had brought with me. Mom was a true animal lover so I knew it was the most thoughtful gift I could give her. With the cardboard box bungee-corded to the front of my bike, I rode home with our new duck. Mom laughed and appreciated the thoughtfulness, but I was forced to return it the next day.

"Happy birthday, Jess!" Dad said. He then let me know he had errands to run that morning, but that he'd be back soon. "I'm gonna go cash in the metal I have, and whatever money I make, you can have for your birthday."

"Really?" I was thrilled.

Dad laughed. "Yepp! I'll be back in an hour."

I was elated. I hadn't expected a gift, let alone money, for my birthday.

I decided for the next hour I would keep myself busy while I waited for him to come back home. I went inside and made my bed up nicely and cleaned up a bit.

An hour passed, and Dad hadn't come back yet, but Mom and Dad were always late to everything so I figured I'd allow him another thirty minutes before getting concerned.

But then another hour passed. I sat on the swing out front and read while I continued to wait.

"At least they *remembered* your birthday," Paul said sarcastically.

I laughed. It wasn't that Mom and Dad didn't remember Paul's birthday; they just had it wrong. All these years we had celebrated it on May 18th. It wasn't until just recently that Mom and Dad realized that Paul's birthday was actually on May 30th. And the only reason they found out was because on May 30th Paul's school sent home a birthday card. Mom got on the phone to inform them they were nearly two weeks late in sending him a card and to correct the date they had on file.

"Mrs. Jennings, your son's birth certificate states he was born on May 30th ..." the secretary told her.

Mom continued to tell her that she was mistaken. But after the phone call, Mom dug up a copy of Paul's birth certificate and realized that the school was right. Ten years of the wrong birth date.

Another hour passed as I waited for Dad to come home—and then a couple more. I took a nap to help the time pass by. When I awoke, Dad was still gone. Pretty soon the whole day had gone by.

Finally, right before dark, Dad's truck pulled into the yard. I couldn't decide if I wanted to be mad at him or excited that he had finally come home. However, no more than sixty seconds went by before my anxiousness got the best of me, and I got up to get my birthday money. Dad was unloading tools from the truck as I walked up.

"Do you have my birthday money, Dad?" I asked.

He stood up straight and looked at me. "Sorry, Jess. I wasn't able to bring back very much for ya," he said, disappointed.

All the metal in the truck was gone so I knew that he made money that day.

"Where did all the money go?" I asked.

He continued unloading things from the truck. "There were some things we needed." He reached into his pocket. "Here. There's a few bucks left. You can go get a slice of pizza with Paul."

I grabbed the crumpled up dollars and put them in my pocket.

"Okay, thank you," I said.

Within a few minutes, Paul and I headed over to the neighborhood across the way to get our friends, Michael and Josh. The four of us walked about a mile down the road to a cheap little pizza place. We laughed and had fun like we always did. We ate our pizza, and then we laughed the whole way back, taking the long way home.

About two hours after Paul and I had left, we arrived back at the trailer. The four of us walked into the yard and toward my mother, who was standing outside. Once she saw us, she began walking quickly in our direction.

"You little bitch, where have you been?"

I stopped in my tracks, as did the other three.

"What? I asked her.

She didn't say anything back. Instead, she stepped closer to me and then reached out her hands. In front of Paul and our two friends, Mom grabbed me by the hair with one hand and started to hit me with the other.

"What'd I do?" I shouted as I struggled to get away.

"Don't try to get away from me!" she yelled as she gripped my hair tighter. "You were gone way too long," she said.

She punched the side of my head, then pulled my head back, and slapped my face. I felt stinging instantly across my cheeks and lips. I stood up straight to catch my breath while quickly trying to adjust my shirt and fix my hair.

I looked over at Michael and Josh who had just watched everything. They were silent. I tried to hide my tears and pretend that I was okay. I walked over to them, but before I could say anything, they told me they had to go.

I said goodbye and watched them walk away. My head pounded with pain. I walked inside the trailer, crawled into my bed, and went to sleep.

Chapter 10

I listened to the rain pour as I sat in the room my parents had recently built onto the trailer. They said they needed more space from my brother and me so they made a hole in the side of the trailer and built a large room made up of wooden beams and blue tarps. The tarps cast a sad blue tint to everything in the room while piles of unwashed clothing filled the corners. The carpet was burgundy with dingy gold flowers running through it. It was stained and had rips. Holes were burnt through it, but there was something about it that I still liked.

The many tarps used to make the roof on the room were loose and unable to keep the rain out. The smell of mildew permeated everything. Pools of water formed in the loose sections of the tarp, and in several spots of the room, heavy raindrops fell, forming puddles in the carpet that made a small *thud* with each drop. The room was dark and gloomy, but I enjoyed spending time in there when my parents were gone. I would lie back on the sofa and enjoy the silence.

This room wasn't always quiet or peaceful though. Just a couple of days prior, Paul and I had heard mom screaming so we decided to check on her. When we opened the door, she was sitting on the sofa with a gun to her chin while my father stood in front of her yelling and telling her she was crazy. Scared that we would somehow make matters worse, we stood by quietly. But once our father attempted to rip the gun out of her hands while she held her finger near the trigger, Paul and I became desperate to see her put the gun down. We begged them both to stop, and as we yelled at them, Paul began to cry. With the barrel still held to Mom's face, she and Dad yanked the gun back and forth. Paul cried louder and louder, and I feared at any moment I'd see the gun go off and shoot my mother. I couldn't stand to watch it any longer.

"Let's go!" I told Paul.

I grabbed his arm and pulled him out of the room. We walked into the trailer and sat down. Paul sat across from me crying in frustration. I felt sad for my brother; his face was red from crying, and I could see where the streaks of tears had trickled down his dirty face. We each told each other that we wouldn't live this way anymore, and we promised one another that we would somehow change all of this. We spent the next several minutes talking until we realized there was no more noise coming from the other room.

I peeked inside to check on them, and the gun was now sitting on the floor, and they were holding each other. Within an hour, they were back outside, and it was as if it had never happened.

These were the memories that came to my mind as I sat in this room. However, this day, this room brought me unexpected news and hope. After sitting on the sofa for a while, I suddenly noticed a letter sitting on the other arm of the chair. I didn't know how I hadn't seen it sitting there sooner, but I decided to get up and look at it. I immediately noticed that my name appeared all over the page. The letter was written in my mother's handwriting, and it was addressed to my grandmother. I sat back down and began to read.

> *"I hope you can understand why I did what I did. I had no choice but to leave John and take Jessica. I had to straighten*

up my life. I lost Jeremy, and I couldn't risk losing her too. Life with John was miserable, and I couldn't have Jessica grow up to see her father addicted to heroin and me getting beaten every day. I just couldn't live like that anymore. One day Jessica will know these things but not until she's older. It's what is best for her right now."

After all these years, Todd wasn't even my father. Thoughts raced through my mind so quickly that I felt like I couldn't move. After all these years and all he had done to me, he wasn't even my father. Was this the same John I heard stories about when I was a kid, I wondered. The man who beat my mother? The man who whipped her with his belt?

My eyes scanned the room as my mind processed the news. Somehow this all made sense to me. It was like I had always known somehow that someone like Todd couldn't be my father. I felt relief. And I wondered if this was my chance to leave all of this. Perhaps after all these years, John had changed. I folded the letter back up and placed it on the arm of the couch. I went on with my day as if I had never seen it.

Days passed, and I spent my time imagining what John was like. I imagined that he had gotten off drugs and that he was a better person than he was when Mom was with him. I was sure that he had a real job too, not digging metal out of dumpsters or stealing parts off of people's cars. And I imagined that every day he thought about me and wondered where I was.

One week later, while we were visiting Mom's friend, Cathy, I decided it was time to tell her that I knew about the letter. I had been waiting for a time when I thought Mom could handle the news without getting too emotional or upset with me. Mom was usually in a good mood when she was hanging out with Cathy.

I walked up to the bedroom door and knocked. "Come in!" Cathy shouted. I could hear Mom and Dad coughing in the background. I opened the door. "Mom, can I talk to you?"

She passed the joint over to Dad. "Sure," she said as she stood up.

I walked into the living room, and she followed behind me.

"What's goin' on?" she asked.

I paused for a moment. I suddenly became nervous.

"I have something to tell you, but I don't want you to get mad at me."

"What is it?"

"I found something in your room."

"Okay." She hesitated, but her voice was kind.

I proceeded to tell her all about the letter and how I found it. I didn't, however, express any excitement about meeting John. I didn't want to scare her by making her think I wanted to leave her.

"Jess, of course I wouldn't be mad at you. You should be mad at me," she said softly. Tears began to well up in her eyes.

"I'm not mad, Mom. I understand." She sat down and put her head in her hands.

"I was just trying to be a good mom," she said under her breath.

"I know. I'm not upset at all. I promise."

She was silent for a moment, then looked up.

"I don't even have a clue where he could be; we haven't spoken in years. I don't even have contact with any of his family."

Suddenly, I felt deflated.

"I need to let your dad know," she said softly.

She stood up and slowly walked back to the bedroom. I walked over to the dining room table and took a seat. I was upset with myself for being excited about meeting John. I had just assumed that once I told Mom everything, she'd get on the phone and call him. The thought never crossed my mind that she wouldn't be able to.

I heard Dad come out of the bedroom. He walked up and took a seat in the chair next to me. I could feel him looking at me as I looked out of the window in front of me.

"You're *my* daughter," he said. "I've raised you so I'm your dad."

I kept quiet and looked down at the floor. After a long pause, he leaned in closer to me.

"Do you understand? I love you. It doesn't matter who your real dad is, okay?"

Many things came to mind of what I wanted to say, but I didn't express my real feelings. Instead I just said, "Okay."

I kept my eyes down, but I could feel him looking at me still. The silence between us made me suddenly realize that, more than anything, he was scared.

After all the years of abuse and secrets, and the guilt I felt because he was my father and I was supposed to love him despite all of it, we were both suddenly confronted with the reality that I had no obligation to keep his secrets any longer.

He stood up from his chair. "I love you, Jess."

I kept my gaze down at the floor. "Love you too."

But he didn't walk away. Instead, he stood quietly next to me, hoping I would say something more that would put his mind at ease.

"Can I have a hug?" he asked me.

Reluctant, I stood up and gave him a hug. When pulling away, I glanced up at him just long enough to see the look on his face. He looked tense and afraid. I sat back down, and he stood there for another moment. He hung his head low. He let out a heavy sigh; then he finally walked away.

Chapter 11

Life continued on as normal after telling my family about the letter. I had decided that in an effort to retain some normalcy for my brother, I would treat Todd the same, and I'd continue to call him dad. Paul, in fact, was the one to take the news the hardest. When he found out, he burst into tears and wouldn't speak to anyone of us. He was devastated and thought that he and I were no longer brother and sister. I assured him we were and that would never change. Still, he kept quiet. Finally, I pestered him enough with my immature jokes that he couldn't help but laugh. After this, the conversation never came up again.

I was worried again about my mother. She wasn't sleeping at night per usual. It was only after three or four days of being up all day and night that she would finally crawl into bed and sleep. But it was the nights that she *did* sleep that I feared she would never wake up. Between the drugs, drunkenness, self-mutilation, and the constant stress, I was afraid one day her body wouldn't be able to take it anymore. Even in her sleep, she wasn't at rest. Every night that my mother slept, she woke up from night terrors. Waking up in the middle of the night to the sound of her screaming was something we were all very used to and had been for years. Sometimes when her screaming didn't stop, I'd get up to check on her. Her body would flail violently, and she'd sweat profusely while screaming at the top of her lungs. From a distance, I'd reach for a part of her body and begin to shake her. I'd have to do this several times before finally she'd wake up. Then, within minutes, she'd be back to sleep. Because of this, whenever Mom was actually getting good sleep, we all did our best to not wake her unless we had to.

Day-to day-life had always been unpredictable, and Paul and I always knew chaos was waiting right around the corner. Even in the rare moments of quiet or calm, it was impossible to not be on guard, waiting for the next crisis to take place and prepared to triage any situation.

However, what I didn't expect was my mother packing a bag and leaving us. I woke up one morning to find it rather quiet. Mom wasn't sleeping, and she wasn't outside. Dad said he didn't know where she was. I thought nothing of it until the day was over, and she was nowhere around. Finally, Dad admitted that in their heated argument the night before, she threatened to leave and never come back. He was starting to think that maybe she meant it.

Days passed, and Dad was stubborn so he didn't bother looking for her. Then a week passed. Soon, an entire month had gone by, and we hadn't seen or heard from her. Mom didn't trust a lot of people so she didn't have many friends. When we checked in with the friends she did have, they hadn't spoke to her. We had no idea of where she was or where else to look.

Worry came over me occasionally, but I knew, more than likely, she was okay and that she left because she wanted to. She was unhappy, and she had been for a long time. I guess I wasn't that surprised that she was gone.

Over the past few months the abuse from my father had been taking place less often until, suddenly, it stopped completely. And now, with Mom not around, a lot of other things had changed also. There was no more yelling, no more waking up in the middle of the night to find my mother hurting herself or in a pool of her own blood, and no more Heineken bottles busting through my window while I slept. All of that had stopped, and to be quite honest, as much as I loved my mother, the thought of her coming back worried me.

Both Paul and I felt slightly more at peace, only as long as we didn't let ourselves think of her. Only when the day had come to an end and we were alone, did we admit to one another that we were worried about her.

But, one morning after Mom had been gone for nearly three months, a tan Ford van I had never seen before pulled into the yard. Dust filled the air as it drove in quickly and then came to an abrupt stop in front of the trailer. Mom hopped out. I walked over, and as I did, she glanced over at me but didn't say a word or even acknowledge me standing there in front of her. I was surprised and slightly hurt. Just then, I saw Dad approaching her. I stood by, curious about what she would say to him.

It turned out that she had spent the past three months with a man. The one that owned the van and who, she said, was there for her in ways that Dad wasn't.

"He's there for me when I need him, unlike you!" she shouted.

Dad screamed at her, defending himself and all that he had done for the family. But this time was different; my mother didn't yell back. She turned around and walked toward their room while Dad followed her, demanding answers. No more than a minute later, she was walking back to the van with some belongings in her arms. Dad shouted at her, but she just slid open the side door of the van and threw her stuff inside. Then she shut the door, hopped in the driver's seat, and sped off, leaving nothing but dust behind her.

With Mom gone, Dad spent much more time away. He said he was recycling metal and doing other things to make money, but we never really knew for sure. However, with no adults around, Paul and I found new ways to entertain ourselves. One night, while left alone, I grabbed the keys to the old Nissan Pulsar and dangled them in front of Paul. "Wanna have some fun?" I asked mischievously.

Of course Paul never passed up an opportunity to be reckless, so, with a nod of his head and a big smile, he followed me outside. We got in the car, turned up the radio, and drove out of the yard.

In-between our yard and the busy main road was a long, paved driveway. Along that driveway was the shop that owned the yard we lived in, along with many other businesses. At this time of night, all of the shops were closed so we drove the car down the long driveway out to the main road. Once on the road, I turned the car around.

"You ready?" I said to Paul while revving the engine.

He laughed as he buckled his seatbelt. "I'm ready!" he shouted.

I pressed my foot to the gas pedal, and we took off! We sped past the dark, empty buildings through the parking lot. Just before leaving the paved driveway and through the chain link fence, I looked down to make sure I was going fast enough for the next part. As we raced through the fence and entered our yard, we could now hear the loud sound of the gravel under our tires.

"You ready?" I shouted again.

Paul laughed as his right hand gripped the handle of the passenger door.

"Here we go!"

I took my foot off of the gas pedal and pulled hard on the emergency break. The car spun around and around. Dust filled the yard, and as the spinning came to a stop, we laughed hysterically. This quickly became our favorite pastime, and we did it every night we were left alone.

As soon as the exhilaration wore off, Paul and I headed back out toward the street to do it all over again.

"You ready?" I shouted again as if it were part of the routine.

While grinning from ear to ear, he yelled back, "I'm ready!"

I pressed my foot on the gas pedal, and we were off! Through the empty parking lot, past the closed businesses, and through the fence once again. This time going faster than I had ever gone.

"Here we go!" I yelled, then I pulled up the emergency break. We could hear the loud gravel sliding under the tires as we started to spin. Only this time, something was different. I was caught between excitement and sudden panic. I had waited too long to let off the gas and to pull the break and the fifty-foot-long tractor trailer right ahead of us was much closer than it should've been. The steel overhang of the trailer lined up perfectly with our windshield and our heads, and it appeared that the car was going straight toward it. It all seemed to be slow motion yet happening too fast. The closer we slid to the trailer, the more I felt completely helpless.

I leaned back in my seat and braced myself for impact. The car continued to spin, and I held on tight while squeezing my eyes shut.

Then the car came to a stop, and it was silent. Without saying a word to each other, Paul and I sat up and looked ahead out of the windshield. The hood of the car was underneath the trailer, leaving only a couple inches of space between us and the metal overhang. I turned to my right to look at Paul. He was just inches away from being smashed. I felt horrible and irresponsible. I looked out of my window to see the clouds of dust swirling around us.

Never again, I thought.

Finally, Paul looked over at me and began to laugh. For a moment, I wasn't sure if I were ready to laugh about it. I was thankful he was okay, but I was shaken up and remorseful. He continued to chuckle until, together, we erupted with laughter.

We carefully parked the car in the spot it was in before; then we placed the keys back on the trailer counter. With our fair share of excitement for the day, we called it a night and spent the rest of the evening talking to each other from our beds.

Chapter 12

It was dark, and Paul and I had just come home when Dad told us that he knew where Mom was. He said that he heard that Ron, the guy mom ran off with, was living in a trailer that was parked in a secluded, industrial area just two miles away from us. It had now been another month that Mom had been gone, and Dad decided he was tired of waiting for her to come back home.

"Get in the car," he told us. I could tell by his tone he was upset.

We got in the car, and within five minutes, we were there. I couldn't believe the whole time she was so close.

In an effort to go unnoticed and to sneak up on Mom, Dad went in the back way, which was through a dark, empty business park. He turned off his headlights, and we slowly drove past large cement buildings lit by tall, orange lights placed at each corner. The rows of cement buildings lined old railroad tracks, and on the other side of those tracks, there was another business. That other business was where Dad expected to find Mom and Ron.

We made our way to the very back of the business park, and we saw the van. Immediately my heart began to race, and as we drove up, we saw my mother stepping out of the passenger side. She glanced over at our car pulling up, and then she shoved something underneath her seat. Her eyes were wide with panic, and by the large sores on her face, I could tell she had been using drugs heavily. Before the car had a chance to come to a complete stop, Dad threw the car into park, causing the car to rock back and forth a few times. He jumped out and approached Mom. Just then, Ron, who we didn't know was there, stepped out from the other side of the van. Paul and I cautiously got out the car, prepared to intervene in any way that we could.

"What're you doin' here, huh?" Ron shouted.

Dad yelled back while throwing up his arms, encouraging Ron to take the first swing.

Paul and I stood by helplessly. We knew there was no way he or I could do anything to diffuse what was about to happen. Within seconds, Dad and Ron were rolling around on the ground, hitting one another. Somehow, after all the fights that Dad had been in, this was the very first one I had ever witnessed, and to my surprise, it didn't seem to be going anywhere. Besides rolling around on the ground and grunting, there wasn't much action. Neither of them were making much contact, and I felt slightly embarrassed that Dad wasn't doing better. After all, this was the man who had taken Mom away from us. Just then, a patrol car pulled up quietly from around the corner.

Thank God, I thought.

The cop put his patrol car into park and calmly stepped out. Dad and Ron got off of one another and stood up.

"Well, what's goin' on here?" the officer asked in a rather calm and amused tone.

Both kept their answers short.

"Nothin', officer. Just had a misunderstanding is all."

The officer didn't pry, and in fact, it seemed he had more interesting places to be and was easy on the two men.

"Can you two agree to squash this and go your separate ways?"

"Yeah, officer. No problem at all."

"Yeah, I'm gettin' outta here," Ron said.

The officer took a good look at the five of us standing in front of him.

"Okay, well, I'm gonna watch y'all leave here, and be safe tonight; no more trouble."

Since my brother and I were young, we had watched our parents have countless run-ins with law enforcement, and they usually didn't end this way. I wasn't sure if it was a good thing he let them off so easy since I knew Ron and Dad would undoubtedly continue this squabble after the officer left.

The cop got back into his patrol car and waited to watch Ron and Mom leave. But then Ron yelled at Mom, and so she decided she wouldn't go with him. The van and patrol car drove away together. Suddenly, it was silent. For the first time in months, the four of us were back together, and we didn't know what to say to each other. I could sense Mom's sudden unease as she stood face-to-face with us after all this time. But, as usual, the quiet didn't last long.

"You think you can just up and leave your family and never come back? What kind of wife are you! What kind of mother are you!" Dad shouted. His blood was boiling, I just knew it.

Dad then got in her face and began screaming at her. I thought, after all these years, I was finally going to see him hit her.

For once, my mother didn't have much to say. She didn't back down from him, but she didn't look so self-assured anymore either. He continued to yell at her while she just took it. A part of me couldn't help but feel some satisfaction from watching my mother being put in her place. It was about time.

Abruptly, Dad stopped yelling at her, turned around, and began walking to the car. Paul and I stood by confused.

He got in the driver's seat and turned on the car. He sat still in his seat and glared at Mom through the windshield while he revved the engine. I could see the hate in his eyes. He mouthed something to her, but I couldn't make out what he was saying.

"What's he gonna do?" Paul asked.

"I don't know, but I'm gettin' outta here." Mom turned and began walking away. Then Dad slammed the car into reverse.

"Is he leaving us here?" I asked Paul.

Then the car tires screeched as he slammed on the brakes. I could hear the sound of the engine revving high as he pressed one foot on the gas pedal and one on the brake.

He was staring right at her. Then he let off the brake and headed straight for her. He was going to plow the car right into her. With nowhere for her to hide in the large empty lot, Mom was completely helpless. She thrust her arms out in front of her, begging for him to stop the car.

"Todd! Stop!" she screamed.

Paul and I helplessly watched, wishing we could help but not knowing how. Paul began to cry.

"I hate them!" he screamed.

When the car was close enough to her, my mother dashed to the left, knowing the car wouldn't be able to get her. Again, I heard the high-pitched whine of the transmission as he sped backward into reverse.

It felt like something out of a nightmare, like Dad was hunting her. He laughed maniacally as he chased my mother across the parking lot. She darted erratically from left to right as she ran, trying to be missed by the car. The tires skidded as Dad swung the car around to then chase her down in the other direction. I didn't know how much longer she could run from him before being ran over. Dad would let off the gas briefly and then rev the engine loudly like a mad man. It looked like it was a game to him now.

Across the parking lot was a small tree. I saw Mom making her way toward it. It didn't look strong enough, but she was going to try to use it to shield her from the car. But I couldn't stand by and watch anymore. I ran toward my mother as fast as I could. I could hear Paul screaming at me to stop, but I couldn't. I saw Mom's face lit up by the headlights of the car while she stood trembling behind the tree. I ran past the car and toward my mother. I stood in front of her as my eyes were blinded by the headlights beaming on me. If Dad wanted to run Mom over with the car, he'd have to run me over too.

In that moment, it was hard to tell what he would do, but in my heart, I didn't think he would hit me. He revved the engine and screamed at me from inside the car.

"Move!"

"No!" I yelled back at him.

"Move!" He pursed his lips together tightly as he glared at me. I could hear my brother crying, and my mother screaming behind me. But I didn't care what happened to me. I didn't want to live this way anymore.

Dad held one foot on the gas and one on the brake. The tires squealed, and smoke filled the air. He wanted to scare me. He was angry with me for what I was doing. The car began to inch forward, and I prayed he would let off the gas.

Then, like a prayer quickly answered, he took his foot off the gas pedal, put the car into reverse, and took off.

"Oh thank god!" Mom cried as she came out from behind the tree. The three of us stood in the dark, catching our breath.

"Jess, damn it. I can't believe you did that." Mom's tone sounded mad, but I knew she was thankful.

"Well it worked, didn't it?" I said back to her.

We were incapable of doing or saying much at that moment. We sat down on the ground and spent the next few minutes getting ahold of ourselves.

Then, after several minutes, we noticed sirens. But not the normal sirens we were used to hearing off in the distance late at night. What we were hearing were multiple sirens coming from all around us. Mom panicked; she was certain that the sirens were coming for us.

"Hide!" she shouted.

We didn't know this yet, but there were several patrol cars heading our way down Weston Road, which led to the business park we were in. We ran through the parking lot searching for a place where we could all hide, but all there was were concrete buildings and the small rows of bushes that lined them.

We ran over to the nearest row of bushes. We slid our bodies behind them as branches scratched our faces and arms. The tops of the bushes were cut short, and the bottoms were cut high, which made our shoes and ankles easily seen. I knew if anyone walked over here, we'd be found quickly. The space behind the bushes was tight so I wiggled my body to try to find a more comfortable position.

The sirens were getting louder; I knew they were close. Our bodies were contorted so uncomfortably in order to fit, but we knew we had to be still. Just then, we heard the patrol cars hurry into the lot, one after the other. Despite all the empty space around us, they parked their cars right in front of the bushes we were hiding in. Several police officers got out of their cars just feet from us. We couldn't make the slightest sound or they would hear us. We couldn't move no matter how badly our legs hurt.

The discomfort was unbearable. All of my weight was on my left leg while my right was bent, and my back was pressed hard against the concrete wall behind me. My head was slightly turned to the left, just enough so the leaves weren't in my face but tilted enough so I could still watch the movement on the other side of the bush. I felt ants crawling up my arms, and I had begun to feel the pins-and-needles sensation as my leg fell asleep.

"The mother was right over there with the two kids when Officer Vargas rolled up on 'em," I overheard one of the officers say.

They *were* looking for us. I couldn't believe they hadn't seen us yet, and as much as I hoped they wouldn't, it would've probably been the best thing for us. The only way Paul and I would ever have a better life was if we were taken from our parents.

A few minutes later, an officer began walking toward us. *This is it*, I thought. I watched his flashlight scan the ground near us. I sat as still as I possibly could. He got closer, and then slowly scanned the bushes with his flashlight. Then he stopped.

My legs tingled painfully, and I could feel the stinging of the ants that had crawled up my arms and neck. My body was begging me to stand up.

I heard the boots of another officer walk in our direction. *Did the other officer signal him to come over?* I wondered. I knew at any moment we'd be instructed to come out from behind the bushes. I braced myself and started a countdown from five in my head.

Five. Four.

The officer's boots stopped, then turned in our direction.

Three. Two. One.

Just then, both officers turned around and went back to their patrol cars.

"Alright. Well, let's keep our eyes out for 'em tonight."

"Alright. Will do."

A few other things were said that I couldn't make out. Then, shortly after, we heard their car doors each shut, and the police were driving away. I knew in that moment that the three of us felt the exact same thing: disbelief.

How is it possible they didn't see us? I wondered.

"Can we get up?" I whispered.

"Not yet," Mom whispered back. She wanted to be sure they were all really gone.

Then, after hiding painfully in the bushes for close to twenty minutes, we were told we could get up.

Although all the sirens had stopped, we could still see red and blue flashing lights reflecting off the buildings around us. The lights seemed to be coming from the front entrance of the building that Ron lived behind.

We looked around, then cautiously made our way through the parking lot, constantly looking in every direction and preparing to hide again if we needed to. We walked over the tracks to where Ron's trailer was. Mom instructed Paul and I to hide while she walked up the long, dark driveway to the entrance. There was a large commercial dumpster on wheels that was just high enough for Paul and me to crawl under. We lay down underneath it and waited for her to come back.

A while passed, and by now, it felt like we'd been hiding for over an hour. Mom returned and told us we could come out. "But be quiet. There's cops all around here," she warned. We could still see the red and blue lights flashing on the buildings.

This time, I got to my feet a little slower than the last time I was hiding. Tiredness had set in, and Paul and I were exhausted. We made our way to the trailer just a few yards away. Mom opened the trailer door and peeked her head inside. The lights were on, but there was no one there. We walked in, and Mom cleared a space for Paul and me to lay down. Mom was wired and didn't need a bed since she didn't plan to sleep that night.

Chapter 13

I woke the next morning right as the sun was coming up. I sat up, looked around, and didn't see Mom. I got up and wandered outside. A couple minutes later, I found her. "Morning, Jess," she whispered. She was still paranoid there could be police around. She and I walked back into the trailer. Paul woke at the sound of us coming inside then we decided to leave to get something for us to eat.

Later that day, Mom received a collect phone call from Ron. He was in county jail and he was calling to tell her about the accident that took place the night before. Mom was told that the sirens and flashing lights were from an ambulance and cop cars responding to a fight between Dad and Ron. After Dad left Paul and I in the parking lot, he drove to the front entrance of the yard where he hoped to find Ron. And he did.

Dad parked his car, then reached under his seat for the only weapon he had with him at the time: a thick metal chain. Ron saw Dad coming toward him with the chain in his hand so he reached into his van and grabbed the only weapon *he* had: a hammer.

Ron stepped away from his van with the hammer in his hand. While cursing and threatening one another, both men walked toward each other with their weapons. Dad swung one end of the chain back and forth to instigate the fight. They stepped toward each other, each muttering curses under their breath, until finally, Ron pulled his arm back and threw the hammer.

Dad's body fell to the ground. The hammer broke through his skull. Ron rushed over to him and called 911. Blood as thick as molasses poured from Dad's head as Ron frantically explained to the dispatcher what had just happened.

The old steel claws of the hammer had gone through Dad's skull and into his brain, immediately causing him to go blind. But suddenly, Dad sat up. With both of his eyes closed and with his legs stretched out in front of him, he used his hands to carefully feel the ground all around him. He was searching for his chain.

"I'm gonna kill you," he told Ron.

Ron remained on the phone, telling the dispatcher everything. Minutes later, an ambulance and police arrived on the scene.

Those were the flashing lights we were seeing.

Dad was kept in ICU, and two days later, he underwent brain surgery. He would then remain in ICU for another week.

Within a couple of days of being in the hospital, Dad's sight had come back, but we were told by the doctor that he would spend most hours of the day sleeping, and it was unlikely we would speak to him while he recovered. He lay unconscious in his hospital bed with his head wrapped in white bandages while Mom cried and held his hands. It seemed this accident had made her realize she still loved him. She kissed his hands and whispered to him how sorry she was for everything she had done and that she loved him very much.

My mother insisted she would take responsibility for Dad's care and that we'd all live as a family again once he was out of the hospital. She wanted to make their relationship work this time around. And as selfish as it may have been, I couldn't have been more against this. Over the months that they were apart, life was a little easier. And the secrets I had felt like less of a burden since Mom wasn't around. I didn't want to go back to the constant chaos and lies we all kept from each other.

About a week later, Dad was released from the hospital, and the three of us picked him up. Since Ron had been arrested Mom had taken his van. We then drove back to our yard. As we pulled up, we saw a group of men throwing all of our belongings in the trash. Turns out that since they hadn't seen Dad or any of us lately, they thought we were long gone. These men were sent to throw away our stuff and clean the area. When we got there, we were told our time there was up, and there was no staying. So the four of us grabbed what we could and moved into Ron's van.

After Dad's surgery, he could still function and do some things; however, the accident left him with an obvious speech impediment and a general sense that he wasn't all there.

Mom was helping him recover, and as the days went on, it seemed like they were happy again. It looked like they were going to stay together this time. I played scenarios over and over in my mind of how I'd tell my mother the truth about everything. The day was coming when I wouldn't be able to hold it all in anymore.

Chapter 14

The following week, I woke up to the sound of Mom and Dad rustling through the cab of the van. As I lay on the floor, I could see out of the windshield that it was another overcast and gloomy day. I sat up and rubbed my eyes.

"Mornin'," Mom said to me from the passenger seat.

"Morning."

"We're gonna head over to the Pick-n-Pull so your dad can get a part for a truck he's workin' on."

"Okay."

I looked over to see Paul curled up in his blanket still asleep.

"Alright, let's get going. Hopefully I don't run into that jerk that was workin' there last time," Dad said under his breath as he hopped in the driver's seat.

I sat quietly during the bumpy ride to junkyard. The blankets we had for cushion provided minimal padding so with every bump, I could feel the hard, cold metal under my butt. About fifteen minutes later, we arrived.

"I should be out in fifteen minutes," Dad told Mom.

He hopped out of the van and headed across the gravel parking lot. Mom watched him as he walked.

I scooched up closer to Mom until I was centered in-between both of the front seats.

My heart was beating out of my throat, but it was now or never. I was going to finally tell her.

"Mom, I have something important to tell you." She looked over at me suspiciously.

"Okay … What is it?" she asked.

I looked over at the gate to make sure Dad was out of sight. Then I looked back at her.

"It's a secret that I've had for a long time. But you have to promise you won't do anything to get yourself in trouble no matter how mad you get, okay?"

She paused and looked at me carefully. I couldn't tell if she were curious or angry. Perhaps it was both.

"You promise?" I asked again.

"Yes," she said. It didn't matter; we both knew in the end Mom would do whatever the hell she wanted to.

I looked up at her. "Dad is a pedophile."

There was silence. We both looked at one another. I was braced for the moment she inevitably erupted with rage and violence. I waited another moment, and she didn't say anything so I continued, "He started touching me when I was five. Well, that's the earliest I can remember."

I paused again and looked at her. She still had the same pensive expression on her face.

"I didn't want to break up the family; that's why I never told anyone."

She turned her face away from me and peered out of the windshield.

"You always said you'd kill someone for touching me. I was scared you'd go to prison and Paul would lose his dad," I continued.

She let out a long, tired exhale. I imagined she was overwhelmed. She sat there quietly like a ticking time bomb. I waited nervously for what would happen next.

She repositioned herself in her seat and gazed out toward the metal gate that Dad had walked through.

Just then, I saw him walking out of it. He was hardly gone ten minutes. I quickly retreated to the back of the van. I rubbed my hands together nervously while I kept my eyes on my mother. She watched him closely as he approached the van. I felt terrified, but at the same time, I felt free, freer than I had ever felt before. I knew in that moment that no matter what the outcome was, I had done the right thing.

The van door opened, and Dad hopped in.

"Well, that was easy, and that jerk wasn't there either!" he said as he placed a metal part and his tools down on the floor.

My mother was silent, but Dad didn't notice anything was wrong. He started up the van, and we headed toward the road. A few minutes later, through the sound of the radio, I could hear the two of them talking about swinging by the Jack in the Box drive-through to get us some food. Life was now coming back to my mother's face, and it looked like she had snapped out of the trance she was in.

My body rocked back and forth with the movement of the van as I watched my mother in the front seat. I was tense, and, without realizing it, I bit my nails down to the skin. I exhaled and told myself that, no matter what, it was the right choice to tell her.

However, I went back and forth between accepting whatever may happen and also being angry that my mother seemed, so far, to be okay.

I sat on the floor as my body rocked back and forth with the turns of the van. Paul was still sound asleep next to me, and for the rest of the ride, I wouldn't take my eyes off my mother.

Several hours passed, and it seemed that she'd disregarded what I had told her. She and Dad were not only speaking, but they were laughing with one another. There wasn't one particular way I wanted her to handle the information I gave her. I just wanted to know she cared and was going to help me. After all of my mother's misdeeds and shortcomings, I was sure this would be how she redeemed herself and made up for it all.

But everything remained the same. As my brother and I sat in the back of the van, I could hear Mom and Dad flirting with one another, and my mother laughing at his jokes. I felt betrayed by her. I'd spent years shoving all of the secrets and anxiety down because I wanted our family to be happy. I had suffered and felt ashamed for so long, but it seemed that none of that mattered, and I didn't know how to cope with that.

That night I lay awake in the back of the van while Paul was sound asleep next to me. We still didn't have enough blankets to cover the entire floor so I could feel the cold metal touching the skin on my back. We were parked at a job site that Mom and Dad had been working on for a couple days; they were painting a four-bedroom home that sat empty. I looked at it from the window and daydreamed about living there. I had never lived in a house that didn't have wheels under it. And as everyone else slept, I lay awake, imagining what life would be like to live normally in a home like the one I could see from the van that I was living in. Suddenly, I heard whispering. I held my breath so I could hear what was being said.

"I love you too," Mom said to Dad. I could hear the sound of her nose sniffling. Then I heard them kissing.

I was angry with my mother. My heart beat faster, and I took deep breaths to calm myself.

Then the whispering stopped. But not a minute passed before I noticed the van was moving. And I realized what was happening. They were having sex.

I wanted to say something. I don't know why I didn't. Instead, I loudly rustled the blankets and rolled over, which made them stop. I kept to myself the next day.

Within a few days, Ron was released from county jail, and Mom decided that she had changed her mind. She didn't want to be with Dad; she wanted to be with Ron. That day, she was gone.

It was back to just being the three of us, and with nowhere to stay, we took our things and went to Dad's brother, Uncle Rick's house. But because it was already a full house, we were only able to stay for a few days. After that, we spent the next couple weeks bouncing around from place to place until finally we were sleeping in our car. Each night, Dad would back the car up into a dark parking lot, hoping it would be a quiet place where no one would see us sleeping. And although it was quiet, I could never sleep. Our legs were cramped, and there were never enough blankets to keep us warm.

After the accident, Dad couldn't work like he used to. Although he was a prideful man, he decided we'd finally apply for financial assistance. He needed my help for much of this. Dad had never learned to read or write. Mom tried to teach him over the years, but it was something he was never able to learn. When I was a kid, I watched him sound out the words on his birthday and Father's Day cards every year. Sometimes, when Mom wasn't around to help him, he would ask me what things said. So after the brain injury, not only did he face the challenge of being illiterate, but now the speech impediment made understanding him difficult. Many times, people couldn't make out what he was saying. Now when he sang along to music in the car, it was like listening to a toddler sing along to a song they didn't know the words to.

Over the next few weeks, there were many appointments that had to be attended and paperwork that had to be filled out, and Dad wasn't capable of doing these things on his own. With Mom gone, he needed someone else to help him. Instead of starting my freshman year in high school, I was tending to these needs.

After a couple of weeks of sleeping in our car, we began staying at an old motel on Mission Boulevard. It was a well-known spot for prostitution and drug deals, and every now and then, we'd see patrol cars parked out front. Cockroaches crawled along the windowsills and the bathroom floor, and the parking lot was home to a litter of stray cats. At night, we would hear arguing coming from the rooms next to us. But as much as all this should have bothered me and Paul, it didn't. We were happy enough to have a bed to sleep in and a hot shower every night.

But, like most things, living there didn't last long, and after staying at the motel for a couple weeks, we left.

Months prior to this, while Dad was waiting at Paul's elementary school, he met a guy named Derek who was standing outside to pick up his daughter, April. Derek was a drug dealer, and while he and Dad were waiting outside, they got to talking. Long story short, we were now moving out of the motel and into Derek's house in San Leandro.

It turned out that Derek's house wasn't actually his but his mother, Linda's. Derek lived in the garage out back where strangers came and went at all hours of the day. Linda spent her days rocking in her recliner, chain smoking and watching soap operas. The acrid smell of cigarette smoke had permeated every corner of the house. But Linda was a caring woman and always made sure that Paul and I were eating enough food.

After a couple weeks of living there, life was feeling a bit more stable, and despite some of my things being stolen by one of the druggies that was in and out of the house, I was still grateful to be able to live there.

Chapter 15

Weeks passed, and I still wasn't attending school. By this time, I had missed so much of my freshman year that I would've been far behind the rest of the students. My days were kept busy with helping Dad get around, making phone calls for him, and attending appointments. Helping Dad became my daily routine, and I was fine with that. Until one day when I didn't want to do it anymore.

I was walking toward the kitchen one evening when Dad stopped me in the hallway outside my bedroom.

"Hey, Jess." He had a smile on his face, and it looked like he had been drinking, even though that was something he rarely did.

"I appreciate everything you've been doing," he said to me. He leaned in close so I stepped back until I could feel the wall behind me. "I know since your Mom's been gone, you've had a lot on your plate." He raised his arm above my shoulder and placed his hand against the wall.

"Yeah, but it's okay," I said. I was nervous someone would walk by and see us standing so close.

"I want you to know that I love you," he said in a low voice.

I looked down at the floor. "Love you too." I tried to make some space between him and me, but the back of my head was pressed against the wall behind me.

"I just wanna make sure you know how much you mean to me," he continued. Then, he leaned in for a kiss. I quickly turned my face away. He paused and looked at me. Then he sighed as he let down his arm and walked away.

Dad doing this to me caused a whirlwind of emotions to come up. I was upset, and I needed to get away. With only a couple of dollars in my pocket, I grabbed a sweater and left. I decided to somehow get to Union City to find my mom. I didn't know what I'd say to her, but I longed to see her. I was told the week before that the van she and Ron were living in was impounded and now they were living in the empty trailer of a semi-truck in a dark industrial area. With only a vague idea of where it was, I set out to find it.

It was starting to get dark and I'd been walking for about twenty minutes when a shiny, black Cadillac slowly drove by. The driver, a guy in his mid-twenties, looked at me as he drove past me; then, he turned around and pulled up alongside of me.

"Hey." He smiled. "Would you like a ride somewhere?"

I knew better than to talk to guys like this. "I'm okay, but thank you." I continued walking, but he continued to drive beside me.

"My name's Victor, I'm not tryin' to bother you, but you look like you need to get somewhere. Let me take you."

I was smarter than this, but I was also upset and eager to find my mother. "Well, I was heading to the bus stop on Hesperian Boulevard. I need to get to Union City." I told him.

"Ya know what?" He laughed. "I'm actually headin' that direction. Hop in."

Against my better judgment, I got in the car.

"So what're you headin' to Union City for?" he asked.

"To see my mom."

"Oh, okay. I hope you don't mind. I just need to make a quick stop before we head out."

"Oh, okay, sure," I replied.

About five minutes later, we arrived at a house in San Lorenzo. Victor stepped out, then leaned his head into the window of the car.

"We're picking up a friend of mine; do you mind gettin' in my backseat?" he asked.

"Uh, okay."

I got in the backseat and sat there as the sky got darker. I decided if he didn't come back out within two more minutes, I'd leave. Just then, he walked back to the car. Nearly fifteen minutes had gone by.

Two friends came out behind him. One of them got into the backseat with me. He didn't make eye contact or say hello. The other sat up front, then finally, Victor got in the car.

"Hey," he said over his shoulder, "we just gotta make one more stop. Then we'll finally be on our way."

Frustrated, I agreed. Ten minutes later, we'd arrived at the second house. Victor honked the horn, and seconds later, a guy walked out and approached Victor's side of the car. He leaned in and whispered something, and then he walked away.

"Alright. We're gonna take Jake's car so we'll fit better," Victor told us.

It was now dark. I got out of the car, and then I got into the back seat of a black Expedition. I began to feel uneasy; something in the pit of my stomach told me this was a bad idea. I turned to the guy sitting on my right. "I think I'm just gonna walk from here."

"No, you can't leave now," he said playfully.

His response made me more uncomfortable. I looked out of my window. The streets were dark, and I wasn't familiar with the neighborhood we were in. Just then, I felt the guy move closer to me. I looked over at him as he placed his arm around me, then his other hand on my thigh. I discreetly unclipped my seatbelt.

"What're you doing?" I asked him.

"We're about to give you what you want." He leaned in and whispered in my ear, "And all four of us are gonna have a turn with you."

My heart beat violently.

"No." I looked up at him. "Take me back."

He looked angry. I wondered if he'd run after me if I ran. Just then, his grip on my thigh loosened.

"Fine," he said. "I'll tell Victor to take you back."

He got out and slammed the door behind him. Now that I was alone, I could've ran, and maybe I should have, but I chose to stay. I refused to walk through a dark neighborhood I didn't know even farther away than where I had started. He at least owed me a ride back to the bus stop I was originally heading to. Just then, Victor walked back to the Expedition.

"I'm takin' your ass back. Get in the car," he said, annoyed.

I walked over to the Cadillac and got in. Victor got in the driver's seat and slammed the door closed.

Before I could finish putting my seatbelt on, he pressed his foot on the gas. He went right through the stop sign and weaved quickly around the street corners.

"Where's that bus stop?" he asked.

I told him where to go, and minutes later, we pulled into a parking lot on Hesperian Boulevard.

"Get out," he said.

I stepped out of the car, and Victor sped off. I was angry, mostly at myself.

It was dark, and I was standing in a parking lot waiting for the next bus to come. I hadn't eaten, and behind me was a Little Caesars, but I could either get a slice of pizza or buy a bus pass. With my stomach rumbling, I chose the bus pass.

While on the bus, I thought about how much worse that night could've been. I didn't know why Victor agreed to take me back instead of doing what he had planned, but he did. I was upset with myself for being so reckless.

Forty-five minutes later, I arrived in Union City. It was 10:00 p.m. I stepped out of the bus onto Whipple Road, and I began my search for my mom.

I felt the wind of the cars speeding past me as I walked the busy street. I was used to being alone and out at night, but I was nervous. No one knew where I was, and I was walking into an area I knew I shouldn't be. Still, my anger toward Todd was enough for me to keep going.

Tall orange street lights tinted everything under them and, soon, there were no other people or cars around. About half a mile up the road, I turned right. At the end of the long dark road was the building my mother was supposedly living behind. I looked ahead. The street was black, except for the occasional street light, and it was silent.

To my left and right there were large buildings with narrow alleys behind them and large empty parking lots. I heard noises, and each time I would quickly look all around me, only to find nothing was there. Several minutes later, I reached the set of train tracks that cut the road in half. As my feet crossed over the metal, I looked down the tracks into the darkness. There was nothing but trash scattered on the ground and shadows. Then, at the sound of something close, I ran. Finally, I reached the end of the road and ran into the pitch-black parking lot. I was all alone back here. Everything was still and quiet except for the breeze blowing in the trees. I looked all around me and continued to walk behind the building, hoping and praying that I would find my mother there.

I proceeded slowly and cautiously. *What if this isn't where my mother is and I am alone back here?* I thought to myself.

I turned the corner of the building and walked into more darkness.

Just then I spotted the container.

"Mom?" I called out. I could see a dark figure moving in the shadows.

"Mom?" I called out again.

"Jess? Is that you?" I felt a swell of relief.

"Yeah, it's me." I could faintly see her walking toward me.

"How the hell did you get here?"

"I walked."

"Oh my God." She turned around. "Ron!" she shouted. "It's Jess. She just walked all the way down here."

"I wanted to see how you were doing," I told her.

She let out a long sigh. "Well, were doin' alright," she said softly. She walked over to the empty trailer, and I followed her.

"This is where we've been stayin'."

Inside the container, and all around it, was pure darkness. There was no heat, no electricity, and no bathroom. I couldn't believe they were living this way.

"Yeah, after we lost the van, we had no place else to go."

"Well, I'm gonna have to stay here with you guys tonight. I won't have a way to get home later," I said to her.

"Oh, okay." I could tell by her voice she was surprised but glad.

For the next ten minutes, I walked with my mother as she gathered some extra clothing that she could use as blankets and padding. Mom had me hold out her lighter so she could see as she made me a bed for the night. For the next twenty minutes, we talked to each other in the dark until I told her I was tired.

That night I went to sleep in a cold metal container using old clothes as my pillow and blanket. The next morning, I took the bus back to San Leandro.

Chapter 16

While living at Derek's, I began noticing a guy named Jay that was coming over to the house a lot. He didn't fit in with the rest of the crowd that normally visited, so it was easy to notice him. The usual visitors to the house were drug addicts, but I could tell that he wasn't. He was muscular, and handsome with dark hair and dark eyes. By the way he dressed and the cars he drove, he appeared to be successful. Each time he arrived at the house, he was driving something different; sometimes a sports car or other times a motorcycle or one of his trucks.

Finally, I asked Stephanie, Derek's sister, who lived in the room across from me, who he was.

"Oh, Jay? Oh, all the girls around here like Jay." She laughed. "He's an old friend. He owns his own construction company and he comes by to see if Derek needs work."

"Oh, okay. He seems like a nice guy."

"Yeah, he is! Everyone around here likes him," she said.

"Okay. Well, I was just curious."

"Sure you were," she teased.

A few days later, I was in the kitchen and saw Jay pull up to the house. I walked out to the garage where Todd and Derek were so I could run into him. I stood in Derek's doorway, making small talk, until I heard him walk up behind me.

"Hi." He smiled. "I'm Jay."

"Hi, I'm Jessica."

"That's my daughter," Todd chimed in.

"She's *your* daughter?" Jay jokingly asked Todd.

I laughed. I spent the next few minutes with the three of them until I decided to go back inside.

"Alright. Well, it was nice to meet you, Jay," I said.

"Nice to meet you, too. You should hang out with us more often," he joked.

"I will," I said back to him.

I walked inside, and about ten minutes later, as I sat on my bed, Jay peeked inside my bedroom.

"Hey, it was really nice to meet you," he said.

"Yeah, it was good to meet you too!"

"I'm gonna be back here tomorrow. I'll make sure to come in and say hi if you're here."

"Okay."

"Alright." He smiled. "I'll see you tomorrow."

"Okay, I'll see you tomorrow."

I suddenly had something to look forward to. From this day forward, Jay never left without coming inside to see me. It made me feel special, like he knew that I didn't belong there either.

The next few days, whenever he came over, he came inside to say hi and make small talk with me before he left.

"So, if I had to guess, I'd say you're, what, nineteen?" he asked while standing in my doorway.

I smiled. "No, actually, I'm fourteen."

He gasped and then let out a big laugh.

"It's okay. I'm used to everyone mistaking me for being older."

"There's just no way!" he said as he continued to laugh.

I didn't find it strange that Jay would flirt with me. Older guys always flirted with me; most of the time because they assumed I was much older than I was.

Soon, Jay started showing up to the house every day, even if Derek weren't there. As time went on, he began to compliment me more. He would tell me that I was beautiful and joke that he couldn't believe I was related to Todd; he didn't know yet that I actually wasn't. Soon, Jay confessed that he knew Derek wasn't home, but that he was coming over specifically to see me. He'd ask me questions about my life; things I enjoyed doing and what plans I had for the future. I felt like he took a true interest in me and I liked the feeling of being noticed by a guy like him.

One evening, after Jay had visited with Todd and Derek in the garage, he walked into the house.

"Hey!" he said with a big smile. "You wanna run some errands with me?"

"Really?"

"Yeah, let's go!" he said excitedly.

"Okay."

I got up and walked to the backyard to tell Todd I was leaving. Jay came with me. Todd was leaning back on the couch smoking weed with Derek.

"I'm gonna go with Jay to run some errands," I told him.

It took him a few seconds to stop coughing and to be able to respond. "Uh, I guess so." He looked at me, then at Jay.

"I just thought I'd get her outta the house for a bit. Plus I could use some help while I'm out," Jay chimed in.

"Okay."

By his pause and leery expression, I could tell Todd was caught off guard and didn't like the idea of me hanging out with Jay.

When I hopped in Jay's truck, I noticed his license was sitting on the arm rest along with some papers and receipts. Trying not to be too obvious, I carefully slid the papers over just slightly so I could see his birthdate. He was in his thirties. This made him over twenty years older than me.

I was attracted to Jay because he was so different from anyone else in my life. He was strong and confident, and he had an air of power about him.

We spent the next couple of hours driving through Hayward as Jay made stops to different places like the bank and job sites. We had conversations about my mother and I shared with him the story of Todd's recent accident and surgery. We also joked and laughed a lot.

We had been gone a while, and it was starting to get late when suddenly Jay pulled the truck over to the side of the road.

"What're we doing?" I asked.

He paused for a moment, and then he unbuckled his seat belt. Then, suddenly, he leaned over and kissed me.

"I've been wanting to do that since the day I met you," he said.

I leaned back in my seat.

"I just feel like I've known you for years," he said.

I looked over at him and paused. "I feel that way too."

"Good." He smiled as he looked at me longingly. He pressed the gas pedal, and the tires kicked up dust as we sped out of the gravel and back onto the road.

We spent the next hour driving aimlessly through town while listening to music, and sharing stories with one another. The mood became serious when Jay said he wanted to share something very personal with me. He told me that, about three years ago, he was released from prison where he had spent several years. He seemed regretful of his past, but he said he wanted to be honest with me.

Jay had been an illegal drug manufacturer. Eventually, after becoming successful at it, he was caught and sentenced with felony drug charges. He served eight years in prison. But I wasn't scared of Jay or bothered by his past. Everyone I had ever known had a past they weren't proud of, and I was sure that if the people in my life would've had the opportunity, they would have done the same thing.

About an hour later, we pulled up to the house.

"I'd hug you, but I don't want anyone to get any ideas." He laughed.

I looked back at him, not sure what to make of everything that had just happened that night.

"That's okay. I understand," I said.

"Okay, well, I'll see you tomorrow."

We smiled at one another, and I got out of the truck. Once I stepped in the house, I heard him drive off. I walked to my room while trying to hide the smile on my face.

A few days later, Jay came over to the house to tell Todd that his schedule was so full that he needed help with invoices and taking phone calls. Jay asked him if he'd be okay with me riding along with him a couple days a week. He agreed.

Chapter 17

The next couple of weeks, instead of spending my days in school, I spent them riding along with Jay. I soon realized there were no invoices he needed help with or phone calls for me to make; he just wanted my company. We drove all over town visiting his job sites and checking on his crew. This didn't take him much time so we spent most of the day out of town. We'd eat at nice restaurants, go to movies, sit in his truck and just talk, and sometimes we'd go to his place. He told me he was happy when he was with me and how he had never met anyone else like me.

Things had gotten serious between us, and I felt like I could trust Jay. I began telling him more about myself and the family I was a part of. I explained to him that Todd wasn't my father and how before living at Derek's, we were living out of our car and motels.

"I wish I could take you away from all this and take care of you," he said, and I believed he meant it.

Jay had a good understanding of our situation, and from that point forward, he always gave me money when were together. It was important to him that I had money for anything I may have needed.

Over the next couple of weeks, Jay and I spent almost every day together. And after seeing how much he cared for me, I decided to tell him about the sexual abuse. I told him that I'd spent the past nine years hiding it, but how recently I had opened up to my mother about it. I also told him about the recent incident in the hallway and how I feared the abuse would start again.

"I wish more than anything I could just get away from him," I said, frustrated.

Jay was quiet.

"I don't want to see you live like this any longer," he said.

"Yeah, well, there's nothing I can really do about that."

"Come live with me," Jay said to me.

"How would I do that?"

He paused for a moment, and his eyes scanned the floor.

"Run away," he said. "You can live with me, but no one can know, not even your brother."

"Really? I don't know. I'd feel horrible leaving Paul."

"I don't think there is any other way, Jess, and I want to take care of you. No one here is looking out for you."

Never in my life had I known anyone like Jay. He was so kind and only wanted the best for me. I couldn't help that I was in love with him.

I wanted to live with him, but I was scared, and I felt so guilty at the thought of leaving my brother. We had been through everything together up until that point.

I agonized over the idea for several days. Eventually, however, I began to believe it was the right thing to do. I knew Paul loved his dad. They were best friends. I knew he'd get over me being gone. I also knew that he was in a safer environment now that he lived at Derek's. He was eating regularly and attending school. He didn't need me anymore.

Later that day, as I sat on the porch, thinking about everything that Jay and I had talked about, I watched Paul ride up on his bike with his friends. They all laughed as their bikes pulled into the dirt driveway. *See, he's just fine without me,* I thought to myself. I decided that I'd do it. I'd go live with Jay.

After talking about it, Jay and I decided I'd leave the following day. That night, I thought about how life would soon change. I lay in my bed, questioning whether I was making the right choice or not. After lying awake until the early hours of the morning, I fell asleep.

It was a Saturday morning, and Paul was already gone by the time I showered and got dressed. I didn't know where he was, but I prayed he wouldn't come home that day. I wouldn't be able to look him in the eyes and lie to him about where I was going. I knew it would be so much easier if he just stayed gone. And he did.

Finally, I got a call from Jay, and it was time. I walked out of the back door to avoid talking to Derek's mom. My heart was racing. I knew I was never coming back. I walked a few minutes down the road and then saw Jay's truck waiting for me. We smiled at each other as I walked up.

I opened the door and hopped in the backseat to be discreet. "We're actually doing this," I said.

"We are," he said back. His smile reassured me that I had done the right thing.

"Did anyone see you leave?"

"No, I left out of the back door, and Paul and Todd were already gone."

"Okay," he said.

Then we drove off. I looked out the window while listening to the loud sound of Jay's diesel truck taking me away.

Over the next few minutes, I was torn between guilt and excitement. But I reminded myself that this was what I had to do. Jay told me that doing the right thing wasn't always easy, but I had to do what was best for me. I supposed he was right. I threw the guilt aside and decided to feel good about my choice.

The first couple days of living with Jay was a dream. I had no responsibilities or worries. And I was happy. In fact, I was happier than I had ever been in my life.

By day three of being gone, I knew I had to let someone know that I was okay. I wasn't ready to talk to Todd so I called Derek's house phone where I knew his mom would pick up. I told her to let Todd and Paul know I was okay, but that I wasn't coming back.

"Your dad is worried sick about you!" Linda shouted at me. "Do you know that he's filed a missing person's report? He thinks you could be dead somewhere!"

"Well, tell him that I'm okay, but I'm not comin' home until I'm ready."

I could hear Linda shouting at me as I hung up the phone. I knew she didn't understand why I left, and I didn't blame her for being upset with me.

Chapter 18

Over the past several weeks, Jay had been staying in hotels. He had just sold his house, and with work bringing him to all different areas, he wasn't sure where he wanted to live permanently. He owned another home, but he had given it to his mom, who lived in the house with her sister. This meant that he and I would be staying at a hotel until we figured out where we'd live.

We did this for a couple weeks before moving in with his friend Eric who owned a condo in San Bruno. I didn't know much about Eric except he was addicted to online gambling, and it was how he spent all hours of the day. In fact, this is what he did for a living, and he was good at it, sometimes bringing in thousands of dollars each week. He was a nice guy, and I wondered if he knew much about me. He was quiet and didn't talk to me much, and when he and I did speak he seemed uncomfortable.

As the days went on, I began to question everything again. I was one month away from my fifteenth birthday. I wondered how this relationship could possibly work when I was three years away from being eighteen. By now, I was so emotionally attached to Jay I couldn't bear the thought of losing him, and after leaving Derek's house, I completely relied on him for everything.

In the weeks leading up to me moving in with Jay, he confided in me about a past relationship he had. About three years earlier, when he was first released from prison, he got involved with a girl who got pregnant just two months into their relationship. Jay had a two-year-old daughter. However, the daughter was abducted by her mother and taken to Mexico. Jay said that the mother was schizophrenic and that she suffered from a slew of mental health issues, which put his daughter in danger.

Jay had hired private investigators, but they were never able to locate the mother or any of her family. For this reason, Jay frequently took trips down to Mexico himself to look for her. And now it was time for Jay to take another trip. He spent a couple days thinking of different ways he could take me with him, but it was too risky. Law enforcement had been notified that I was missing, and we couldn't take any chances of me being found with him. So I stayed at the condo with Eric while Jay was gone for a week.

After Jay had been gone a couple of days, Eric invited me to a movie with him. By this time, he and I had gotten to know one another a little more, and I was comfortable spending time with him. I felt like he was a kind-hearted and innocent guy.

After arriving at the theater, Eric put the car in park and sat there quietly for a moment.

"I wanted to tell you something … between us," he said. He didn't make eye contact with me, and based on the long pause, he seemed nervous.

"Okay."

"I just want you to be careful, okay?" he said as he looked up at me. His sudden seriousness caught me by surprise.

"With Jay. Be careful," he clarified.

I looked back at him, and I didn't know what to think about what he'd just said. He didn't want to elaborate, and I didn't ask him to.

"Okay," I responded.

"Okay then!" He reached for the door handle and quickly got out of the car.

I knew it took courage for Eric to say what he did. Jay wasn't someone you messed with, and if he had known about this conversation, it would've been bad for Eric. I didn't say a word about it. This comment made by Eric did cause me to reflect on my relationship with Jay, and when I was honest with myself, I did question us being together because of my age. However, I had brought this concern to Jay before, and he explained to me that he'd spent so much time in prison that he felt he missed out on a lot of his life. He said that, mentally and emotionally, he felt much younger, like how young he was when he went in. Because of that, he couldn't help the way he felt about me. Jay said it was actually a common way of thinking for those who had spent time in prison. After this, I felt like I understood him in a way that others couldn't.

A couple more weeks passed, and the glamour of my new life began to fade again, and the guilt came back. I felt ashamed for leaving Paul, and I longed to see my mother again. I knew she loved me, and I knew the drugs were responsible for her behavior. I needed to know she was okay so I decided that morning I'd find her. I called Uncle Rick.

"Ya know your dad is lookin' for ya," Rick's wife Beth said to me. "He filed a missing person report."

"I know he did, but I'm not goin' back home."

Beth didn't pry. After all, she and Rick had expressed their frustration in the past about how Todd and my mother weren't taking care of Paul and me the way they should've been. I knew she didn't blame me for leaving.

It turned out that my mother had called Rick and Beth a few days prior and left a phone number where we could reach her. Later that day, I called her, and we arranged to meet the next day.

At about 1:00 p.m. the following day, Jay and I left San Bruno. He drove me to Hayward where I'd meet mom at the Taco Bell at Jackson Square.

I walked inside and scanned the room. My mother sat in a booth to my left. Her hands were folded on the table as she looked out of the window. Her blonde hair was dirty, but I could tell that she had tried to style it nicely for our visit. She had large, red sores on her face, and her acid-wash jacket was stained with black grease. She sat politely with her two scuffed boots pressed tightly together. It was comforting to see her, and it didn't matter how dirty and strung out she looked; she was my mother.

Her eyes looked up at me, and I saw her face light up. Her eyes were gentle, and her lips were pursed. She looked nervous.

"Hi, Jess," she said softly as she got up to hug me.

"Hi, Mom." I hugged her back lightly. "Let me get us some food," I said. I knew she probably hadn't eaten all day. We sat across from one another, enjoying our meals and small talk.

"Jess, where are you living now?"

"I'm safe, Mom. That's all I wanna say right now," I said gently.

"Jessica, I'm your mother. Don't I deserve to know where you're living and that you're safe?"

"I *am* safe, I promise. But I know that if I tell you, you or Todd will show up and ruin everything." My tone was soft but direct.

"Okay," she said as she let out a heavy sigh. "I don't like not knowing where you are, but I understand." She looked down and fumbled with the napkin between her fingers. She looked sad.

After our meal, we walked together outside.

"I really don't like that I have no idea where to find you." Her voice cracked as if she were about to cry.

"I know, Mom, but I promise I'll see you soon."

We walked together to the corner of Jackson and Amador. We hugged each other, and then I reached into my pocket and gave her a twenty-dollar bill so she could get herself some food later.

"Thank you, Jess. I love you."

"I love you too, Mom."

We both turned and walked away, not knowing the next time we'd see each other again. On my way home that day, I decided I would finally make myself heard. I was going to make sure that my mother and everyone else knew about Todd and the sexual abuse.

Chapter 19

A few days had passed since I visited with my mother. When I left her that day, I was determined to prove to her, and everyone else, what Todd had done.

It was getting dark, and I was sitting in Jay's truck as he drove us to a house in San Lorenzo that I gave him directions to. Todd had spent a lot of time at this house over the past few months, and I hoped that this night, I'd find him there. It had been weeks since I had seen or spoken to him.

As we approached the house, I saw Todd's car was parked right out front. I was relieved yet nervous. We drove past the house, then turned down a side street where Jay let me out.

"Double check that it's turned on," he said.

I had put a small tape recorder in my purse. I checked to make sure that the red light was on and that it was recording.

"Good to go," I said.

I shut the truck door and began walking down the street toward the house. For the first time since I was six years old riding in that old Chevy truck, Todd and I were going to talk about the molestation.

I felt my heart pounding through my throat. I was fearful of how he'd react when he saw me standing at the door.

As I got closer, Todd walked out of the house and toward his car. I looked down at the recorder to make sure I could still see the red light and that the microphone was pointed up. I watched him walk back to the front door and then immediately back to the car with recyclable metal in his arms. I expected he'd noticed me at any second.

I approached the trunk of the car. I stood there for a moment, waiting for him to notice me. I watched him struggle to stack everything in the back of the car until finally he lifted his head out of the trunk.

"Where the hell have you been?" he yelled as he threw up his hands. His eyes were wide, and there was no doubt he was fuming with anger. But I wasn't going to let him control this conversation or scare me. I was there to make him listen to *me* for once.

"I had to leave. I couldn't live with you anymore," I said calmly.

"What the hell are you talkin' about?" His voice was loud, and I was sure everyone around could hear him.

"I didn't want to live with you anymore."

"You didn't want to live with me? I work hard every damn day to take care of you and your brother! What do you mean you didn't want to live with me?"

"You know what I'm talking about." I paused. "Everything you've done to me since I was a little girl. I remember all of it."

His eyes were wide, and he stared at me, speechless. He looked at me as if I were crazy.

"I don't know what the hell you're talking about! You have lost your mind, just like your mother!"

"I'm not crazy. I remember all the nights you came into my bed and took off my clothes." My body started to quiver as I spoke.

"Whoa! You have lost your damn mind!" He began to frantically shove more metal into the car. "I can't believe my own daughter would make up a lie like that!"

"It's not a lie, and you know that." I looked at him, but he wouldn't look at me.

For the next several minutes, I told him that I remembered everything he had ever done and how I had lived with shame all of my life because of it. He continued to deny it all.

"You're a damn liar! You're just like your mother! You need mental help." He began laughing psychotically.

I continued to calmly recount memories of the molestation while he frantically adjusted the pieces of metal over and over again. Then I paused and stood there quietly for a moment.

"Did you do those things because you loved me or because you wanted to hurt me?" I asked him.

He lifted his head out of the trunk of the car and looked at me. He was silent, and we stared at one another.

"Did you do those things because you loved me or because you wanted to hurt me?" I repeated.

His body slumped over. He looked to the ground, then back up at me.

Tears rolled down my cheeks, and for the first time, I felt the pain of these memories coming over me. The truth was that I didn't care to know his reason for doing what he did. Nothing mattered to me except proving to my mother that this really happened.

Todd sighed heavily. "No, I didn't do those things to you to hurt you. I loved you, and that's why I did them."

I stood silent, staring back at him.

"I'm so sorry. I love you so much," he said as he stepped closer and wrapped his arms around me. "I'm so sorry for what I did to you," he whispered.

Worried the recorder wouldn't be able to pick up what he was saying, I pushed him away and took a step back.

"I didn't think you'd remember any of it. Sometimes I thought you didn't even know what was happening." Todd continued to explain himself until finally he was silent again. After a few minutes of this, there was nothing more each of us could say.

"I'm gonna go," I said to him.

"Wait, what're you talkin' about? You're just gonna leave again?" He raised his voice again. I suppose he thought that I'd come back home now.

"This doesn't mean everything's suddenly okay. I'm not coming home."

He looked me in the eyes, fuming.

"Tell Paul that I'm okay, and I'll see him soon."

He looked down at the ground.

"Fine."

I took a long look at him before I turned around and walked away. That was the last time I ever spoke to him.

I walked down the street to where Jay was waiting for me. I hopped in the truck, and Jay looked at me nervously. "How'd it go?"

"He admitted to everything."

I wasn't sure how I felt. I didn't know if I were ecstatic or if I wanted to cry after what had just happened.

"Alright, that's good. Let's hear it."

I pulled the recorder out of my purse, placed it on the center console, and pressed play. We listened closely, eager to hear what the recorder was able to pick up.

As I listened, I felt guilt for what I had just done. I realized that a part of me did love him, and there were times that he was a good dad. I knew this recording could put him in prison.

We listened for nearly twenty minutes, and Todd's confession was clear. Now I needed to decide what to do with it.

Once we arrived back home in San Bruno, I downloaded the file onto our computer. I then burned it onto a CD, making three copies. One for me, one for my mother, and one for Rick. It was important to me that they all knew the truth.

The next morning, Jay drove me back to Hayward where I showed up at Rick and Beth's doorstep.

"Hey, stranger," Beth said as she opened the screen door. "What're you doin' here? Your dad's still lookin' for ya."

"Well, actually, I just saw him. I can't stay long, but I have something I need to give to you."

"Okay, come inside," she said. "I'm glad you're okay. We've all been wonderin' about you."

"I know." I smiled. "I'm here because I have two CDs. One for you and Uncle Rick and one for my mom. Please listen to it after I leave, then tell my mom to come pick hers up." I handed Beth two white envelopes that held the CDs.

"Um, okay. Will do, kiddo."

"Thank you. I'll call you tomorrow. Is that okay?"

"Yeah, honey, of course. Give me a hug."

We hugged, and she walked me to the door.

The next day, I called Rick and Beth's house to talk to them about the recordings.

"Your Uncle Rick and I listened to the tape together, and he was so upset he drove down to the police department right after he heard it." Her tone was furious. "The police have the recording now. Honey, we are just so sorry that he was doing those things to you."

I could hear shuffling on the other end and then Uncle Rick grabbed the phone. "Honey, I am so sorry. He deserves to go to prison for what he did. I don't care if he's my brother, you never do those things to a child."

The anger Uncle Rick felt was clear in his voice. But as he spoke, I felt peace. My voice had finally been heard.

"Your mom's coming over tonight to pick hers up," he said.

Days passed, and I didn't call my mother. I wanted her to have some time to think about Todd's confession and how she had disregarded everything I had told that day in the van. And once I knew the police had the recording, I didn't do anything further. I waited to see what would come of all of it.

Living in San Bruno and getting the confession from Todd made me feel like for once I was in control of my own life. And it proved to me that I was better off on my own than with my parents. I decided to do the only thing that made sense: file for emancipation.

Over the next few days, I filled out all of the paperwork, and that following Monday, while Jay was at work, I took a taxi to the San Mateo court house and submitted my petition.

As the days passed, I waited anxiously to hear from the police about Todd's confession and also from the courthouse about my emancipation. I expected to get some news any day.

Chapter 20

Jay was at work, and Eric was out of town for the day, leaving me home by myself. I had just gotten out of the shower and dressed when suddenly I heard a loud knock at the door.

I wasn't expecting anyone, and we never had visitors. I peeked around the corner at the door. "This is the San Bruno Police Department," said a man on the other side of the door. "We need to speak to you."

My hands began to shake. I stood still, hoping that maybe if I didn't answer, they'd leave.

"Open the door." The officer banged loudly.

Somehow I knew they were there for me but I didn't know why. My heart raced like never before. I stood against the wall. I wasn't sure what to do.

"We know you're in there. Open the door!" The officer sounded impatient.

Suddenly I realized what I had done. I used Eric's address when I filed my paperwork for emancipation. I didn't think about the fact that I had been a "missing person" for over two months. Now they knew where I was.

Nervous, I walked over to the door. I knew I had to open it, and it was better for them to show up now instead of when Jay was home. I could see the dark figure behind the peep hole as I approached.

"We can see you, Jessica. Open the door!"

I reached for the handle; my hands were shaking. I opened the door and stepped aside.

Two police officers and a man in a suit from Child Protective Services rushed in.

"Jessica, you have exactly two minutes to gather any belongings you have; then you're coming with us."

I didn't ask questions. I went to the kitchen and grabbed two plastic grocery bags from under the sink.

"Hurry," the officer said sternly. "You have two minutes!"

Tears poured down my face, but I didn't make a sound. I went to my closet and shoved as many things I could into the plastic bags as the police officer stood by and watched me.

"Times up. Let's go!" The officer shouted at me. "Take a seat at the table."

I sat down, and they began their questioning. "Who are you living with?"

"A couple: Eric and Sheila," I responded.

A couple of months prior, Jay placed an ad in the newspaper on behalf of Eric. The ad stated that a couple named Eric and Sheila were in search of a roommate that would be willing to do administrative work in exchange for a room. Because I was so young and unable to work, this was the perfect arrangement for someone like me, which is why he chose to write the ad this way. Also, stating that it was a couple instead of a single man made it less suspicious. Eric was in fact in a relationship with a woman who was at the house frequently, but she didn't live there.

I sat at the dining table, and between the stern voices of the officers and the light fixture above my head, I felt like I was being interrogated, and I was. The social worker questioned me while the officers walked through every room of the condo. I didn't stray from the story I had rehearsed about the ad in the paper. When I was asked about Sheila, I described her as if I had known her for years.

"We will find out if you're lying about any of this so you might as well be truthful. Who lives here with you?"

"I am being honest. We can wait here for Eric and Sheila to arrive, and you can ask them yourself," I answered respectfully.

For the next several minutes, the police officers and the social worker continued to question me.

I told them all that I could without telling them about Jay. I explained that my mother had been gone for months, and that I had only left so I could get away from my abusive stepfather. Still, I felt like I was the criminal.

With my two plastic bags, I walked downstairs to the social worker's car. Both officers walked closely behind me, watching every move I made. The social worker opened the passenger side door, and I got in. I looked at myself in the mirror. I had a large red rash all over my face and neck from crying. I sat in the car and waited while the police officers and the social worker spoke.

Once we began driving, I was informed that I'd be taken to a holding facility where a team of social workers and medical professionals would decide what to do with me. I was told the process could take several days and that I'd be watched twenty-four hours a day.

I watched the choppy waves as we crossed over the San Mateo Bridge. Every bit of energy I had was gone. I didn't want to speak or move. I stared out of the window and wondered what my life would look like from that moment on.

When we reached the other side of the bridge, the thought of jumping out of the car crossed my mind. I thought of all the reasons why I should, but something inside me told me to stay in the car. Images of my brother kept coming to mind. And something told me that if I just went with what was happening, things would eventually get better.

Finally, we arrived at an unmarked building in Hayward, which would be my home until I was released, probably to my mother. We had driven past this building hundreds of times when I was a kid. It didn't have a sign, only large black numbers indicating the address, and all of the windows were tinted dark so there was no way of seeing inside. I had always wondered what this building was and I was about to find out.

Chapter 21

The social worker and I stepped out of the car and walked together into the facility. It was a large open space with bright fluorescent lighting. In the middle of the room was a large desk where the receptionist sat. Behind that was a hallway that led to examination rooms where a doctor would exam me after I was admitted.

The man escorted me to the woman at the front desk. They greeted one another, exchanged paperwork, and he said goodbye.

The woman asked me questions as she checked off the boxes on her forms. Next, she instructed me to go to the back of the room and stand against the wall so they could take my photo. I was given a summary of the facility rules, and I was told I'd be held there until further notice. Next, she handed me off to a nurse down the hall. I answered more questions for her while I waited for the doctor to see me. More than anything, I wanted to call Jay and tell him where I was. I knew when he got home the only thing he would see would be all of my stuff gone. I hated that no one knew where I was.

Cameras were fixed to each corner of the room, watching every move I made. When I used the bathroom, someone went with me and stood next to me. When I showered, someone stood outside the shower curtain while telling me how much time I had left. I still remember seeing the woman's boots underneath the shower curtain while I stood under the hot water. I was given a cot in the middle of the facility where I would sleep that night. I spent every minute lying there, crying quietly to myself. And out of desperation, I began praying.

Hours had gone by since I was admitted, but I was still the only person there besides the staff.

The first night was torturous. Each time I looked up at the clock, it seemed the hands hadn't even moved. Finally, I became so tired from crying that I drifted off to sleep. The following day, I alternated between watching TV and napping, waiting to be released to my mother.

By my third day there, I had only left my cot to use the bathroom or when instructed to go eat in the dining area. The TV in front of my cot had become my favorite thing. It was a distraction from my thoughts.

I lay on my cot and wondered when I'd get to leave and where I'd be living when I did. Then I heard the door open. I looked up and I couldn't believe it.

It was Paul. He was escorted in by a social worker. It looked like he hadn't bathed in a week. I could see the streaks from where the tears fell down his dirty cheeks. His clothes were filthy, and his hair was messy. I couldn't have been happier to see him. I quickly got up and walked over to him.

Together, we walked over to the woman at the desk so Paul could be admitted. Next, we sat down so he could go through the same intake process I did three days prior. I felt a deep aching in my chest as I listened to what my brother had been through while I was gone. I learned that shortly after I ran away, Todd was kicked out of Derek's house. With nowhere else to go, he and Paul slept in the car for a couple weeks, but eventually the car got impounded. After that, they were sleeping anywhere they could. Late one night, the police were patrolling an area when they found an old abandoned van on a dark street. It looked suspicious so they got out of their cars and looked inside. When they opened the back door of the van, they found Paul asleep and alone in the back of it. I knew I'd never forgive myself for leaving him.

Once Paul answered the women's questions and saw the nurse, we were both taken into an office. Inside was a woman who informed us of the process. She told us that living with our mother was not an option because she was homeless, not to mention a drug addict. We were also told that there were no other relatives that they were aware of that could take us.

"So we'll be placing you in either a foster home or a group home. Which would you prefer?"

Paul and I looked at one another, confused. We didn't know much about either one. I took a moment to think about it.

"Can we stay together?" I asked.

"If you choose a foster home, then, possibly."

"Well, a foster home, I guess."

"Okay, foster home it is." She looked down at her paperwork and continued to write.

I sat nervously, hoping I had made the right decision. This was all still sinking in; I had just assumed we'd be released to our mother.

We were to be placed in our new foster home the following day.

Chapter 22

The next day, Paul and I were driven to Modesto. We pulled up to a small, humble house on the corner of the street. It was light brown with a dead front lawn. Around it were tall white Sycamore trees.

We grabbed our belongings out of the van, and our new foster mother stepped outside to greet us.

"Hi, everyone," she said with a smile. "I'm Deborah."

Deborah was an older black woman with large brown eyes and streaks of gray throughout her hair. She looked sweet.

Paul and I introduced ourselves, and then we made our way to the front door with her. The screen door shut behind us and the van drove off.

The walls were stark white and bare. There weren't photos hanging or decor. The home was simple. A boy sat on the living room floor, playing with a toy fire truck. He was our new foster brother, Brian. Brian was a twelve-year-old boy who was given up when he was young because of his severe autism. Deborah took him in several years prior and had recently legally adopted him.

"Well, your rooms are down this way," she said as she led us down the hall.

"Get yourselves settled, then come out when you're ready."

I stepped into my bedroom and set my bags on the floor. I looked around my new bedroom, and I wondered how long I'd be there.

I closed my bedroom door, then I sat down on the bed. This was the first time in days that I had been alone. I held my head in my hands and cried.

I cried as much as I could in that ten minutes, knowing I'd have to hold it together for the rest of the day.

I patted the tears from my face and got up to empty my two bags and hang my things in my closet. I took a deep breath, then stepped out of my room.

After several hours of uncomfortable conversation and long periods of silence, I was thankful to see the sun going down. It meant I could go to sleep soon and be alone again. Even Paul went to his room early.

I took a long shower, then crawled under the covers of my bed. I wondered if I'd be able to sleep that night. I felt myself drifting into a depression that had lain dormant the past couple months. I lay there while my mind wandered into dark places I was desperate to get out of. On my dresser was a small radio. In an effort to silence my own thoughts, I turned it on and moved the dial until I found something calming to listen to. I stopped at a song that sang of God's love for us. I moved the radio closer, then got under the covers. Soon, I fell asleep.

The following morning, I woke in a fog, counting down the hours until I could go back to sleep before I had even opened my eyes.

Over the next two or three days, I began to notice that Deborah was quiet. She had seemed kind and caring when we first arrived, but now she seemed unemotional and standoffish. I started to feel like she didn't care much for me or Paul. Whenever she spoke to Brian, she was friendly and warm, and I could see that she loved him. But the same warmth wasn't felt during our interactions with her. Also, when we were briefed on what to expect in foster care, we were told that we would be supervised twenty-four hours a day, but over the past couple days, she didn't care at all about what we did.

About four days later, I was supposed to have my first day at Beyer High School. But shortly after dropping me off, Deborah was called to come pick me up. The school said they couldn't take me. It was almost April, and I had missed my entire freshman year up to that point. Because of that, I was forced to enroll in a continuation high school—a school for troubled teens and those who supposedly were far behind other students their age.

Each day, I made the two-mile walk there and back instead of taking the bus. I even took the long way at times. I needed the time alone. I needed the space to be lost in my thoughts without having to hide the depression I felt or pretend that I was fine. The time alone forced my mind into the deep crevices where the pain hid. The more time I spent away from others and in my own thoughts, the more I realized how broken I was and how I didn't even know myself.

But, in the midst of my heaviness and despair, I would pray, and when I did I felt brief moments of peace, and hope. So I began to pray often—on my way to school and on my way back. And at night, I'd pour my heart out to God as a way to relieve some of the heaviness and pain I felt.

I was starting my life from scratch. I was figuring out who I was and who I wasn't. I knew that if I ever wanted to heal, I needed to intentionally make choices that helped me grow.

I began running each night. This made me feel not only like a healthier person, but like a normal person. It helped me feel just a little bit more confident in myself. And though it was a small beginning, it gave me something to focus my mind on.

There were times when I felt okay, when I felt my mind was in a quiet place for a moment, but as soon as I became aware of the quiet, all the reasons why I should be worrying rushed back. Obsessive thoughts overwhelmed me. After my father's first visit years ago, dread and anxiety were my constant companions. I had never really known what peace felt like, and I was beginning to see that throughout my life I'd been preoccupied with the chaos all around me, which drowned out all of the chaos that was actually raging within me. Being in a steady environment where there was no constant tumult or calamity to focus on slowly brought my issues to the surface. I was finding that I could no longer run from them.

Several times a week, I experienced panic attacks. I was usually triggered by a man resembling Todd walking or driving by. My chest would tighten, and my body would shake uncontrollably. At night, I'd peek out of my bedroom window to make sure there were no strange cars parked on our street. And if there were, then I was certain in that moment that it was him. I'd lay in my bed trembling, feeling like the world was crashing down on me. The following morning was always the strangest—the brief feeling of calm and the sun shining through the trees. It made me wonder how I possibly felt so hopeless the night before.

My mind never felt at rest, not even when I was asleep. Vivid nightmares haunted me. I had never in my life experienced a nightmare until my first night living with Jay; now they occurred every night. Scenes of blood rushing from my mother's head and me trying to help her but never being able to. Images of demons chasing me or Todd coming to kill me for what I had done to him. Often times, I'd be woken up in the middle of the night to the feeling of evil all around me, like I was being watched by something. I'd squeeze my eyes closed and pray until my heart calmed enough for me to eventually drift off to sleep.

A few days later, Paul and I were driven to San Leandro for interviews with child psychologists. We each spent one hour in a taped interview to examine our state of mind. Afterward, the court ordered that Paul and I attend mandatory therapy sessions once a week.

A couple days later, Paul and I received a visit from our social worker, Curtis. He came to let us know that our mother was checked into a rehab in a small town about forty-five minutes south of Modesto. Once she heard that Paul and I were taken to the holding facility in Hayward, she made the decision to get help. She had been addicted to drugs and alcohol for over twenty years; we had never known our mother sober.

Once the dust settled and I realized that Deborah didn't worry about what I did, Jay and I began to see each other again. It seemed that nothing had changed between him and me, despite the time away and the distance. Seeing Jay put a temporary pause on the depression I felt and helped me to feel happy again. He regularly drove to Modesto and spent one to two days a week with me while I'd skip class to spend the day with him.

Several weeks later, our social worker called Deborah and told her he would drive to the house to check on me and Paul. He said he had some news to share and he would be visiting us the following day.

The next day, I waited anxiously for Curtis to arrive. I hoped he'd bring news that Paul and I would be getting out of foster care.

I rested my chin on the windowsill of my bedroom window, waiting for his car to pull up. I watched the sun shine through the leaves that blew lightly in the breeze. I prayed for good news, and I longed for all these broken pieces of my life to come together in a way that made sense.

Finally, I saw the familiar gray sedan pull up to the house, and before he could park, I leapt off of my bed.

Moments later, I heard the doorbell ring, and I casually walked down the hall as Deborah greeted Curtis.

"Hi, Jessica. Hi, Paul."

"Hi," we said to him.

"Let's take a seat." Curtis motioned us toward to kitchen.

"I'll be in the living room if you need me," Deborah said to Curtis.

We each pulled out a chair at the dining table and took a seat.

"Well, I have some news for you."

I looked at him expectantly.

"We've been searching for family members that could perhaps take you both in, and in our search, Jessica, we located your biological father, John."

"Oh!"

"Yes, so we have coordinated a day for you two to meet one another."

I looked at him blankly, recovering from the feeling of shock.

"Next week, one of our drivers will come pick you up and take you to Oakland where you two will meet and have a little visit to get to know one another."

"Okay … that sounds good," I said. My mind was suddenly racing. Meeting my real father could change everything.

"Yes, we're excited. This could be a very good thing. Okay, well, besides all of that, how are things here?" he asked both of us.

"They're fine."

"Yeah, they're fine," Paul answered.

After a few more minutes of talking, Curtis headed out the door.

"Don't worry. I won't go anywhere without you," I said to Paul. I meant it. I would never leave him again.

"Yeah, you better not."

I walked to my room to digest the news. I was more hopeful than I had been in a long time. This was what I wanted three years prior when I found out that he was my father. I hoped that John could give me, and Paul, a better life. However, I wrestled with the stories I had heard and the things I knew about him.

As the week went on, I became more nervous, and as the day approached, I reassured Paul that I was going to take him with me wherever I went. I wouldn't be leaving him behind no matter what.

One week after my talk with Curtis, I was picked up by a driver and taken to Oakland. The driver, an older man with white hair, made small talk with me while we drove. Normally I preferred to be left alone in situations like this, but it helped the drive seem like less time, and it calmed my nerves. After nearly two hours, we had arrived. We pulled up to a tall silver building. The weather was overcast and much cooler than it was when we left Modesto. The driver opened my door and walked me to the front entrance of the building.

"Ok, well, good luck in there!" he said as he held the door open for me.

"Thank you." I smiled at him, but my heart was racing.

I stepped inside the elevator and checked my reflection in the old scratched mirror. I was in the best outfit I owned: a pair of black-striped capris with black wedges and a red top. I hoped I'd make a good impression.

The elevator dinged as it came to my floor. I took a deep breath, and I stepped out. My eyes scanned the hallways around me as I looked for my room number.

Then there it was: an open door with a plastic sign above it with a small "15" on it. I stood tall and stepped inside.

An older man with long white hair tied back in a ponytail quickly stood to his feet. He wore faded blue jeans and a tucked-in Harley Davidson T-shirt.

"Hi." He nodded his head then diverted his focus to the floor.

"Hi," I said nervously.

He stepped forward and reached his arms out for a hug. We embraced each other loosely, and he lightly patted my back before quickly letting me go. We both sighed simultaneously as we let go of one another.

He stood back and took a long look at me. I was the daughter he hadn't seen in over fifteen years. And he was the father who had an unfortunate reputation that preceded him. We sat down.

"Well, you're not as thin as your ma was."

I looked at him, confused, as though I must've misunderstood him.

"What?"

"I just mean your ma was always real thin, ya know, 'cause of the dope."

"I guess ..." I said defensively. Those weren't the first words I imagined he'd say to me.

He sat across from me, several feet away. I watched him twirl his fingers nervously as he tried to find the right words to say. We had one hour. One hour to say all the things we'd never been able to say. One hour to make up for fifteen years of all the events in each other's lives that we had missed.

We both fidgeted in our seats. The room was cold, and because of the fluorescent lights and tiled flooring, it felt like a hospital waiting room.

His eyes were wide, and he looked like he wanted to say so much, but he didn't. We sat in silence for a moment. Somehow all the things I thought to say had disappeared into thin air. Just then, John began to speak.

He asked about foster care and about Paul. In-between my answers and his questions were moments of silence. He joked about my mother and how her cooking was horrible. I knew he meant to lighten the mood.

"Yeah, your mother." He laughed. "She made me never want to date another woman again."

It pained me to see him so awkwardly searching for anything to say. But I knew the stories of the horrible things he had done to my mother, and the jokes he made weren't funny to me.

He looked down at the floor and rubbed his thumb over the palm of his hand.

"My mom told me about the trailer you and she lived in, in Fremont, the one with the broken windows," I said to him.

"Yeah, you were just a few months old when we lived there. Your ma hated livin' in that trailer with a new baby."

"I lived there too?"

"Yeah, and your ma and I fought all the time. I wasn't very kind to your mother." He looked up briefly before turning his eyes back down to the floor. "I shoulda treated her better than I did."

I watched his eyes scan the floor. I didn't say anything. I didn't want to interrupt this time of reflection for him. It was satisfying for me to know that he did feel remorse for the things he had done.

For the rest of the visit, he told me about his life, what he did for a living, and how he wondered where I was during all those years. He said that he searched for me after my mother ran off but that he soon felt that I was better off without him. I didn't know if I believed him or if it were an excuse, but it didn't matter.

"Well," his head popped up as he changed the subject, "I really wish I could have you come live with me, but I can't." My heart sank. "I live with a roommate, and I don't have the space. I wish I could."

"That's okay, I didn't expect that anyway." But I had.

A few minutes before the meeting was over, John stood up.

"Alright, kiddo. Well, I should get goin'."

I looked up at the clock on the wall. We still had ten minutes left.

"Okay, me too." I stood up to give him the awkward hug we were both expecting. He handed me his phone number, written on a small piece of paper, and we said goodbye. I had waited so anxiously for this visit, and it was over.

Chapter 23

Once a week, the foster care agency sent a driver to our house to take Paul and me to see our mother. But after three weeks of this, I still hadn't gone. Each week the van pulled up to the house; Paul ran outside, and I watched him leave from my window. I wasn't ready to see her again. I loved my mother, sometimes I felt I loved her too much, but it was better for me to keep my distance and not let my guard down around her. I was taught to not need my mother ever for anything, and just because she was ready to be a mother, it didn't mean that I needed one.

Weeks passed, and each time Paul came back from his visit to Atwater, he'd come into my room and tell me how it went.

"Mom says she loves you, and she understands why you won't visit her," he'd tell me.

She was trying to give me space and time to come around. But by the following week, we heard that Mom was found hanging from a rope inside of a shed. The shed was on the rehab's property, and somehow, she was found immediately before she sustained serious injuries. A woman ran into the shed and lifted her up to remove the homemade noose from around her neck while calling for help. I imagined that if she had attempted this inside the house perhaps they wouldn't have found her alive. She admitted afterward that the shed was too flimsy to hold the weight of her body and not nearly tall enough for her to fall from. I thanked God that all she had was that flimsy old shed.

My heart felt heavy with grief as I listened to what she had done. I imagined her placing the rope around her neck and the thoughts that must have been going through her mind to bring her to that moment. I felt a deep sadness for her. I wanted to run to her and tell her I loved her. But I couldn't. I couldn't save her every time she wanted to die. This was the pattern that we had lived in our whole lives: she'd hurt herself for attention, and it would fulfill some need deep inside her, a need to feel loved. This was a battle that she had to overcome.

The following Sunday morning, at around 7:00 a.m. Deborah knocked loudly on our bedroom doors.

"Get up! Get your clothes on! You got fifteen minutes!" she shouted.

I jumped out of bed and rushed to get dressed. I didn't know yet what I was getting ready for, but I did so as quickly as I could. I rushed into the bathroom to brush my teeth and comb my hair, then I stood in the doorway, waiting to find out where we were going so early in the morning.

"*We* are not going anywhere. Me and Brian are," she said, "and I'm not leavin' you two in my house alone."

"What?" I asked, confused.

"Brian and I are goin' to church. You two can wait for us to get back."

Deborah shooed us out of the door as she spoke. The metal screen door slammed shut, then she put her key inside to lock it.

"You want us to wait here?" I asked.

"Yes," she said bluntly.

Paul and I watched she and Brian get into her van and pull out of the driveway. We couldn't believe that she was leaving us outside with no food, no water, no bathroom, and no money. We hadn't even had breakfast yet.

There was nothing for us to do other than sit on the porch and wait for her to come back or walk around town hungry without money, which was exactly what we did.

Several hours later, after church service and brunch with her sister, Deborah arrived back as Paul and I sat on the concrete steps of the porch.

"Hello!" she said as she walked up.

She looked happy and refreshed, which annoyed me. Paul and I, however, were hungry and hot from being in the sun. We stepped inside the house, and we both immediately grabbed water from the sink and drank.

"Why can't we go to church with you?" I asked. I had been waiting all day to ask her that.

"Well, my church is for black people only."

I didn't know what to say so I said nothing. I now felt I was right to think that she didn't like Paul and me.

I carefully considered what I would do if this happened again. I knew that Paul and I were given freedom that we'd never be given in another foster home. Because she didn't care what we did, I was able to see Jay when he came into town, and Paul was able to hang out with friends after school. If I told the social worker about this, they would've removed us and placed us somewhere else. So as frustrating as it was, I decided to let it go.

But each and every Sunday after that, we were woken up and kicked out of the house by 7:15 a.m.

And each time, she'd stay gone even longer than the weekend before. Pretty soon, she wasn't coming home until dinner. Other nights, she didn't come home until almost 9:00 p.m. When I told

Jay about what was going on, he felt horrible and made sure I always had money, giving me a couple hundred dollars every time I saw him so I wouldn't have to worry about not having money on days like this.

The summer progressed, and a couple of weeks later, it was over 100 degrees outside. Being locked out of the house all day was unbearable, and on this day, I had been on the porch waiting for Deborah for hours. I sat hunched over on the concrete steps as my head pounded. I had a headache and excruciating cramps. I didn't have any water or medicine to take, and I couldn't bear to make the one-mile walk to the store. Earlier that morning, I told Paul to go to the park without me. I wanted to just sit and rest. Eventually, Paul came back to check on me then he and I walked together to get food. It wouldn't be until hours later that Deborah would pull up to the house. She had been gone for thirteen hours. I went to my room, shut the door, and went to bed.

Jay's work schedule required him to be in the Bay Area most days, but he continued to visit me on the days that he could drive out. His visits were the only thing I had to look forward to. We'd talk and laugh. We felt just as happy as we did before I left. He assured me that distance wasn't going to get in the way of us being together and that I was the one he wanted to spend his life with.

But within a few weeks, something changed, and our visits didn't feel as happy as before. I began to notice that Jay had a temper; something I hadn't learned in the time that I lived with him. Initially, when he arrived, he was excited to see me. He'd greet me with a big hug and tell me how much he missed me, but then, shortly into the visit he'd become upset over little things that didn't make sense to me. We started to argue about things like him thinking I was checking out other guys. One day, as we were driving, I had looked out of the passenger window at the same time that there was a young guy standing on the street corner, and

Jay yelled at me. It scared me, but this wasn't typical behavior from him so I let it go, blaming it on the distance and time apart.

On my phone calls with Jay, he told me how much he loved me and couldn't wait to see me again. This restored my sense of peace and made it easy to forget about the temper he had during our last visit.

But with Jay's next visit came the same behavior as the last one. Several weeks prior, he had bought me a new cell phone so he and I could easily reach one another, and during our next visit, he asked me for it.

"Let me see your phone," he said.

I was caught off guard by his request. "Okay. Is everything all right?"

"I don't know. I wanna see who you're texting when we're not together," he said casually.

He walked over to my purse and grabbed the phone. Then he took a seat and began scrolling through my call list and text messages.

"Why do you suddenly think I'm hiding something from you?" I asked.

He looked up at me, then back down at the phone. I waited a minute, then I asked him again.

"Why don't you trust me?"

"Shut your mouth!" he yelled.

Tears filled my eyes. I never imagined Jay would speak to me that way. Several minutes passed as he continued to look through my phone. Then, after not finding anything, he put it back in my purse. Then he got on his phone and ordered us a pizza as if nothing had happened. He started to talk to me normally as if he hadn't just screamed at me. It didn't make sense how he could be so upset, then completely fine again. I wanted to talk to him about what happened, but instead I kept quiet, worried that I would just upset him again.

Jay took a long shower, then the pizza arrived. We began to eat together, and he started to crack jokes to lighten the mood. I was desperate for this to be a good visit together; these visits were all I had. I cracked a smile and continued to eat as he told me how busy work had been lately. Then, he pulled out a letter he brought with him that he had written days before.

"… *You're the one thing that keeps me going. I love you more than I've ever loved anyone, and I can't wait to start a life with you.*"

As I read his letter to me, all the negative emotions I had just felt melted away, and I felt happy again.

Later that night, we said goodbye. He wrapped his arms around me and promised to see me the following week.

The following Friday morning, Jay drove to Modesto again to see me. I waited down the street from my high school, where he would pick me up. Within a few minutes, I could hear his truck down the street. Then, there he was.

Everything started out normally, but an hour later, when we left the cafe where we had breakfast, things took a turn for the worst. Suddenly, he became quiet, and he wouldn't respond to me when I spoke to him.

Then he parked.

"Where's your phone?" he asked.

My heart pounded as I realized we were having this dreaded conversation again. I handed him the phone. For the next several minutes he looked through it thoroughly, then gave it back.

"I have this feeling I can't shake. A feeling that you're seeing someone else," he said. He looked over at me suspiciously.

"I would never do that to you, I promise. Why do you think that?"

He stared at me and was quiet. Then, without saying anything more, he put the truck into drive and sped off.

"I know you're seeing someone, Jessica. You don't have to lie to me." He spoke slowly in a low, angry voice, which was more frightening than his yelling.

He was focused on the road as he drove faster than all the other cars around us.

"I promise I'm not lying to you!" I cried.

He kept quiet while weaving in and out of traffic. I was sure we were going to get in a wreck if he didn't stop.

"Please slow down!" I said while holding tightly onto the door.

He continued to drive recklessly, getting honked at by other drivers, until he finally slowed down and I began to catch my breath. For the next ten minutes, we drove in silence. He didn't speak to me, and I was scared to speak to him. After a few minutes, he began to relax again, and shortly after that, he was even nice to me again. I was so relieved that he had calmed down that I didn't say anything about what had just happened.

Despite how Jay was treating me, I never once considered leaving him. He loved me and he had done so much for me, and, despite what had been happening, I was terrified of not having him.

However, a new argument happened each visit. He'd begin by questioning me about what I did each and every day of the week. He wanted to know details like who I talked to during class and whom I spent my lunches with and on which days. These weren't things I recalled right away, and sometimes it required a lot of thought to remember. But as I took the time to think about it, he accused me of fabricating lies to hide what I was really doing. He'd then repeatedly ask me the same questions over and over, telling me that I was lying. This caused me to question my own perception and the things I thought I knew. This behavior started happening consistently, and it became exhausting. However, it never failed that within an hour or two, he'd be back to his happy self again.

I grew used to this new normal with Jay, and to me, the good still far outweighed the bad. But in the weeks to come, things would continue to get worse.

About three weeks had passed since Jay and I saw each other last. I walked a couple blocks away from school where he was waiting to pick me up. I smiled at him as I walked up, but he didn't smile back.

"Hi," I said sweetly as I hopped in the truck. He said hi back, but I could tell by his tone that something was wrong. He didn't seem happy to see me. I buckled my seatbelt, and we drove off.

"Is everything okay?" I asked. But he didn't respond to me. I waited a moment before saying anything more. "Is something bothering you?"

Suddenly he slammed on the brakes and pulled the truck to this side of the road.

"Yes, something is bothering me," he said in a low, angry tone.

A feeling of dread crept into the pit of my stomach.

"Why are you upset?"

"Why am I upset? he shouted. "You didn't think I'd notice?"

"Notice what?"

He looked over at me, seething with anger. He stared down at my neck while his breathing became heavier. Then he used his hand to brush the hair away from my face.

"What?" I asked, worried.

"You have a hickey on your neck," he whispered angrily.

"What are you talking about?"

"I'm looking right at it, I could see it as you walked up to the truck."

I was speechless. There was nothing on my neck. I stared back at him. He paused for a moment, then wrapped his fingers around my neck and shoved my head into the passenger door window. Tears filled my eyes as the side of my face hit the glass.

I held my face in my hand and cried quietly while trying to make sense of what had just happened.

I reached for the rearview mirror to turn it toward me. The only mark on my neck was from where his fingers were pressed into my skin.

"Jay," I said crying, "are you okay?"

He stared out the windshield.

"Jay, there is nothing on my neck," I said, concerned.

"Do you think I'm stupid? I'm looking right at it!" he shouted.

Before I could say anything more, he grabbed my neck and shoved me into the door again.

"What's wrong with you?" I cried. "You're hallucinating or something."

He looked away from me, then slammed his body back into his seat. I could hear his heavy breathing. Then he stepped on the gas. I put my seatbelt back on and gripped the door handle; the tires screeched as we turned the corner. He sped through the neighborhood and swerved around cars.

"Jay, please stop!" I pleaded.

"Shut your mouth!"

He sped around the corners, almost hitting another car.

"We're gonna crash!"

About sixty seconds later, Jay took a left turn and slammed on his brakes. Our truck spun around, doing a complete 360 turn, then stopped within just inches of smashing into the parked car next to us. A man rushed out of the house across the street at the sound of our tires coming to a screeching halt. My hand gripped the handle above the passenger door, and I sat stiffly as I tried to catch my breath. I wondered what was going through his mind. Seconds later, we drove off. We went to a rural part of town where there were orchards and empty fields. Jay pulled the truck over.

"Take off your clothes," he said.

I looked at him, confused.

"Take your clothes off right now."

I looked all around us, then back at him.

"I'm not gonna say it again!" he yelled.

He pushed me back against the passenger door, grabbed my waist, and unbuttoned my jeans.

"If you've been sleepin' around, I'll know."

"I haven't been, I promise!" I cried.

He cursed under his breath as he struggled to rip my jeans off of me, and for the next several minutes, I lay there while he examined me. I closed my eyes. Tears streamed down my face as I waited for him to be done. Several minutes later, he threw my jeans at me.

"Get dressed."

I felt humiliated. I sat up and slid my jeans back on. I sat in the passenger seat and kept quiet. I didn't know who Jay was anymore.

Chapter 24

Two months later, Paul and I were removed from Deborah's. Our newest social worker, Sheri, responded quickly to a call I made to her earlier that evening about an incident that happened with Deborah's eighteen-year-old nephew, Stephen. Deborah left us alone at her sister's house while the two of them went shopping. Paul, Brian, Stephen, and I all sat in the sunroom around the large wooden table, playing cards, when suddenly Stephen became upset.

"What're you lookin' at, Brian?" Stephen asked. His tone caught my attention. I looked over at him.

His hands were folded in his lap, and he stared at Brian intently.

"Nothing. I-I'm looking at the cards," Brian responded nervously.

Brian kept his gaze on the cards in his hands. It was silent. I looked at Stephen, then back at Brian.

"No, Brian. What're you looking at?" he shouted. "You gotta problem?"

Paul and I looked up at one another, confused.

Stephen stood up. "I'm so sick of you, Brian."

Brian looked up at Stephen as he walked toward him. "St-Stephen ..." Brian's voice was shaky.

I realized something horrible was about to happen, and there was no one there to help us.

Stephen grabbed Brian by his neck and threw him onto the ground.

"Stop!" I screamed.

Then Stephen picked Brian up from the ground and slammed him down onto the table. I ran for the phone and called Deborah as I ran back into the sunroom. I told her what was happening and told her to hurry. Deborah was concerned, but she didn't seem as surprised as I thought she should be, and when I asked her if I should call the police, she said no. "We're comin' home now; we'll be there shortly," she said calmly.

Stephen picked up Brian again and threw him back down, this time hard enough for the table to break and everything on it to come crashing down onto the floor.

Once Brian was on the ground, Stephen began kicking him repeatedly in the face and the chest. Suddenly, Stephen stopped and then ran for the door.

I got down on the floor next to Brian.

"Are you okay?" He didn't respond.

He held his head and gently rocked himself back and forth while in the fetal position. Paul was bent down next to me. Our eyes traced the shoe prints imprinted on Brian's forehead and cheeks.

"It's okay, Brian. Your mom will be here in just a minute, okay?" I gently rubbed his arm. Still, he didn't speak.

Within minutes, Deborah and Mary arrived. They rushed over to Brian, who was still lying on the ground.

"Oh, my poor baby. Brian, sweetie, are you okay?" Deborah lifted him off of the ground and held him in her lap. He began to cry loudly as she rocked him.

Within an hour, Stephen was back home. Brian was never taken to the hospital, and Stephen was never arrested. I overheard Deborah's conversation with Mary, and I learned that this had happened before, and Stephen had been placed in a psychiatric facility several times for incidents like this.

I was afraid this would happen to Paul, so that evening I called Sheri. I explained to her what happened, and within hours, Paul and I were removed from the home.

That night, Paul and I were taken to a foster family that we had stayed with once before while Deborah was away for a weekend trip. Their names were Mark and Stacy Johnson. They were a wealthy family that lived in Del Rio, Modesto. They had two children of their own along with four other foster children. With Paul and me, they now had eight children. Four of them were siblings, one of which was an eighteen-month-old little girl named Rebecca. Once I learned her story, she quickly became my favorite person in the house. She, along with her three siblings, had all come from an abusive home. The parents used drugs and alcohol, and oftentimes the kids were starved. I felt that Paul and I had a lot in common with them, although we wouldn't talk about it. I spent my free time playing with Rebecca and helping feed her. Often times, I'd watch her take the food off of her plate and hold it in her hand. When I looked away, she'd shove the food into her diaper. She was so used to starving that she was saving her food.

I thought living with Mark and Stacy would be enjoyable. They lived in a big house, and they told us about all of the fun trips they took and the activities they did together. But life with them was much different from how they depicted it.

One morning, I had an hour worth of chores to do before I was allowed to do anything else that day. I gathered the cleaning supplies, put my gloves on, and started working on the bathroom. I knelt on the countertop as I wiped the streaks from the mirror. I could see Stacy's reflection as she walked into the bathroom.

She paused and looked at me. "Those shorts look gross on you," she said.

I turned around to see her standing behind me.

"What?" I asked.

"Those shorts make your legs look fat. They're very unflattering."

I looked at her for a moment, turned around, and went back to wiping the mirror.

"That's rude to say," I said to her.

"I'm just bein' honest," she said, then she walked away.

Over the next few weeks, the eight of us often witnessed Stacy yell and scream at Mark. His demeanor was always meek, never wanting to further upset her in front of us. He was a kind, quiet man. It confused me why she treated him so poorly.

One afternoon, I was sitting in the backyard, reading, when she opened the back door and quietly called for me.

"Jessica, come here and watch this."

I got up and followed behind her as she walked down the hall toward her bedroom.

"Shh, don't say anything," she said.

We stopped right outside the closed bedroom door. She placed her hand around the door handle, then looked back at me and chuckled. She waited a moment, then threw the bedroom door open.

"Where are the keys to the van?" she yelled.

I had just seen the keys earlier on the kitchen counter. I also watched her shove them inside a drawer.

"Stacy," Mark sighed, "what are you talking about?"

Mark was sitting in front of his computer as he worked from home that day.

"You have the keys. Where are they?"

"Stacy, I put them on the counter like I always do."

"No, you didn't! Now I have to go search for them before I can leave the house!"

Mark let out a heavy sigh but kept his focus on the computer screen.

"Forget it!" she said. She slammed the door and walked away as she began to quietly laugh.

"I had to give him a hard time."

All along she did have the keys.

Shortly after that incident, she had another cruel idea. It was evening right before we were all getting ready for bed. She called all the kids out of their rooms and told us to come into the kitchen. Once all eight of us were in front of her, she lined us up in a row. She began to pace slowly in front of us. We stood barefoot in our pajamas, glancing at one another, wondering what was going on.

"You all need to show more respect in this house," she said as she made eye contact with each one of us.

"Mark and I work very hard to take care of all of you, and you should show your appreciation."

Then she stopped pacing and stood in front of Paul.

"And you!" she said to him. "You need to stop wetting the bed!"

I was speechless. This was a secret Paul tried so hard to hide from the other boys. Every morning, he got up early, before everyone else, to remove the sheets and change his clothes.

Paul burst into tears and stormed out of the kitchen.

"How could you embarrass him like that?" I asked.

I could hear my brother crying as he walked down the hallway to his bedroom.

"Well, I'm sick of cleaning those damn sheets every day! It was time everyone knew!"

I looked at her and wondered what I could possibly say to express how I felt about her in that moment. Instead, I left my place in line and walked out of the kitchen.

"Where do you think you're going?" she asked.

I ignored her and kept walking. I stepped into Paul's bedroom to see him curled up in his bed crying. My heart ached for him. I sat next to him until he told me he wanted to sleep. I said goodnight and walked into my room. Shortly after, Stacy came in.

"This is my house; you have no right to walk away from me when I'm talking to you."

"Well, you had no right to do what you just did."

"You know what? The two of you can leave this house. And you know what else? I bet when your brother's grown, he ends up in prison. And you, you'll be on welfare with a house full of kids, all with different daddies."

I looked at Stacy as she stood in front of me, and despite what she had just said to me, I wasn't even mad at her. I knew she was only trying to hurt me, but it didn't work.

"I don't wanna live here anymore," I said to her calmly.

"I think you're right about that. I think you and Paul should go."

Stacy requested that we be removed from her home, and by the following week, we were gone. With just two weeks before Christmas, Paul and I were moved to our third home.

Chapter 25

We arrived at our new home just a couple days later and we were greeted by our newest set of foster parents, Sherry and Patrick Frizzell. They were a kind, older couple, and they made us feel welcome and comfortable. Despite the short notice they had that we were coming to live with them, they went out and bought Christmas presents, so when we arrived we had a mountain of gifts under the tree.

For the next ten weeks, we lived with Sherry and Patrick. And each day felt longer than the one before it. I was grateful we were put in such a loving home, and I tried to show my appreciation, but no matter what, I couldn't remove this veil of depression over me. Some days I felt okay, and other days I felt like I was slipping further and further with no way to stop it.

February 25th was the last day of foster care, and we were going to be released back to our mother. Our bags were packed and were placed near the door. Paul and I sat at the kitchen table, waiting to see Mom's white Ford Explorer pull up to the house.

I looked out of the window and wondered what this new chapter of life would look like.

There hadn't been a single day of our lives that our mother wasn't under the influence of drugs and alcohol. I didn't know who she was. And Paul and I wouldn't just be adjusting to living with her, we'd also be living with Ron. After everything, they stayed together. They admitted themselves into rehab together and then graduated from their programs at the same time. Now they were living together in a duplex that just happened to be on the same property as the women's rehab.

The clock on the wall had just hit 1:00 p.m. when our mother pulled up to the house. Ron was in the passenger seat.

"She's here!" I announced.

Sherry got up from her chair and headed toward the door to help us grab our bags, and Paul opened the door before Mom and Ron could even ring the doorbell.

"Hi, son," Mom greeted him with a smile.

They hugged as I grabbed my bags.

"Hi, Jess."

"Hi, Mom. Hey, Ron."

Paul and I hugged Sherry and promised we'd keep in touch.

Paul and I transitioned once again to a new home and new schools. I was on my third high school, and Paul was adjusting to living with the same man that nearly killed his father. Even after several weeks, it felt like we were all strangers living in the same house. None of us knew how to talk to one another or what to talk about. When Mom and I talked, our conversations were forced and painfully uncomfortable for the both of us. Getting to know one another would take time.

But Mom did her best. She cooked dinner each night and kept a clean house. She'd come home from the grocery store with snacks and foods she knew Paul and I liked. She'd attend her drug and alcohol meetings religiously several times a week, no matter how tired she was when she got home from work. I knew she was desperately trying to be a good mother.

Despite the distance and time apart, Jay and I continued to speak to each other regularly, and we saw each other when we could.

A couple months after moving in with my mother, John asked if I'd spend a day with him attending a family function in Sacramento. He wanted to introduce me to the relatives that had never met me. John and I had never spent that much time together. I didn't know what we'd talk about for the nearly two-hour drive so I was apprehensive, but I agreed.

That weekend, John made the two-hour drive to pick me up. Mom walked me outside, and, for the first time in sixteen years, she said hello to my father. She was cordial while he avoided eye contact.

I said goodbye to Mom, then opened the passenger door to get in. There was shattered glass on my seat. Turns out he replaced the busted window but never cleaned up the old glass.

"Do you have something to clean this up with?" I asked.

"Oh! Yeah. Sorry." He handed me an old crumpled paper bag from the backseat.

"Yeah, don't worry. I'll clean it," I said, annoyed.

I swept the glass onto the floor while John waited for me to finish. I took a deep breath and prepared myself to spend the entire day with him.

Minutes later, before getting on the freeway, John said we had to make a stop so we pulled into the Tower Mart on the corner. Once he hopped out, I began to look around the car. The backseat and floor was littered with empty Budweiser cans and wrappers.

Just then, I looked up and saw John coming out of the store with one of those brown paper bags in his hand.

You gotta be kidding me, I thought to myself.

"You're gonna drink and drive?" I asked as he got in the driver's seat.

"Yeah a tall Budweiser for the road!" He laughed.

"I don't think that's a good idea."

"Oh, it's fine." He clenched the can between his legs and reversed the car. "Beer doesn't even get me drunk anymore." He laughed.

Once we arrived in Sacramento, we spent the next several hours talking to John's sisters, brother, and his nieces and nephews. He told them stories of what I was like when I was a baby before Mom ran off with me. He said his favorite memory of me was when I was sitting in my highchair, eating spaghetti. I sat there covered in marinara sauce from head to toe. He laughed as he remembered it. This visit turned out to not be so bad after all.

Finally, it was getting dark, and we had to get back on the road. I said goodbye to everyone and felt pleased that I had decided to go. But before getting on the freeway, we made a stop at another gas station. Just like last time, he came out with a brown paper bag in his hand.

"I'm not comfortable with you driving after you've been drinking all day," I told him as he got inside.

"Oh, I'm fine. Promise!" I could tell he wasn't taking me seriously by the grin on his face.

He buckled his seatbelt and started up the car.

"Let me drive," I told him.

"Jessica, are you being serious?" He braked and looked over at me.

"Yes."

"Well, fine. If you say so."

He pulled the car over near the entrance of the parking lot, and we switched seats.

I slid my seat forward, adjusted the mirrors, and began to drive off. I didn't plan on speaking to John for the rest of the drive. But no more than thirty seconds had passed before I was shouting.

As I drove the car around the freeway ramp and onto the freeway, the steering wheel came off. I screamed!

"Oh boy!" John said. He didn't sound as surprised, which was alarming to me.

With a line of cars behind me and bright headlights coming toward us, there was no way to steer the car.

"Just gently press the brake and veer off to the side," John said casually.

The car drifted off to the shoulder, and as I held the detached steering wheel in my hands, I realized John was laughing.

"You should see your face," He chuckled.

"What're you laughing at?"

"Oh, just relax," he told me. I was furious. He had pushed me too far that day, and I was sure I'd never spend another day with him again.

We came to a complete stop, and I could feel the wind from the cars speeding past us.

John reached into the backseat and grabbed a monkey wrench that was tucked behind his seat. He clamped it down on the bare metal piece sticking out where there was once a steering wheel. He then grabbed the loose wheel out of my hands and placed it back on. He had clearly done this before.

"Good as new," he said before erupting with laughter.

"Forget it, I don't want to drive! Just take me home!"

"Alright then." John placed his beer in the cup holder and lifted himself out of the passenger seat.

We switched seats, then got back on the road. For the first couple of minutes of the drive, I could hear small outbursts of laughter, then it was quiet.

Finally, after a long silent drive, we pulled up to the house. "Alright, kiddo. That was fun. We'll get together again soon."

"Yeah, sounds good." But I knew I'd never get in another car with him again.

I walked into the house, breathed a sigh of relief, and then laughed with the family as I told them all about it.

Chapter 26

As the weeks went by, Jay's visits and phone calls became less frequent. He blamed his schedule for us not seeing or speaking to each other, but I couldn't ignore the nagging fear that there was more to it.

Danielle was a girl whom Jay and his mother, Patricia, had known for several years; she was considered family. Danielle had recently started helping Jay with taking phone calls, setting appointments, and writing invoices, like what Jay asked me to do for him when we first met. Not long after they began working together, my phone calls would go unanswered. Sometimes it would take days before I'd finally be able to reach him. When we did finally speak, he apologized for his busy schedule, but he told me that this would be the new normal until things calmed down.

Then late one evening, after days of calling Jay and not being able to reach him, I decided to give it one more shot. I called and finally the phone picked up. However, it wasn't Jay on the other end; it was Danielle. There was an awful feeling in the pit of my stomach.

In a short, unfriendly tone she told me that Jay was busy working late and he wouldn't be able to talk to me. Then, without saying goodbye, she hung up. This brief exchange with her left me more unsettled than before, and not being able to talk to him made it worse. I felt my mind spiral out of control. It wasn't until the following night that I was able to talk to him.

"Ever since Danielle started working with you, you never pick up my calls. Is there something you need to tell me about her?" I asked.

"I'm not dealing with this right now. I'm tired," he said. Then he hung up.

Desperate to talk to him, I called back.

"I'm not having this conversation with you! Stop acting ridiculous and immature. I don't have patience for that."

"Well, will you answer my question?" I asked.

There was a long pause followed by a loud sigh. "There is nothing going on, and nothing you need to know. Danielle is like family to me; I've known her since she was little. Now don't ask me about this again."

After trying to further explain my feelings, Jay just became angrier and accused me of not trusting him. He told me I was acting childish for even bringing it up and that he wasn't going to even want to talk to me if I were going to ask him such ridiculous things. I felt embarrassed for bringing it up, and I ended up apologizing.

Chapter 27

Often throughout the week there were altercations between Mom and Ron. I knew the neighbors could hear the screaming; there was no doubt about it. Dishes were thrown and shattered on the kitchen floor. Mom's collection of glass paperweights became cannons to hurl past each other. Eventually, it would end with Mom threatening to hurt herself.

After more than twenty years of using drugs and alcohol, my mother didn't have the reasoning or communication abilities others did. Her mind was constantly looking for confrontation and chaos. Mom didn't know any way to resolve issues other than becoming violent. And between her behavior and Ron's callousness and short temper, they were a dangerous combination. Frequently, Mom was admitted into the nearby mental hospital, and she was prescribed more bipolar and antidepressant medications than I knew even existed.

Although the drug use had stopped, Mom and Ron still had the same way of thinking that they did on the streets. They had no idea how to talk to one another or have a healthy relationship, and often their fights got out of control.

It became a routine that several nights a week I'd stay up to make sure they didn't kill each other and to make sure that Mom didn't hurt herself. I'd sit on the floor at the entrance of their bedroom, making sure Ron didn't come in and that Mom didn't go out. Foul language was shouted from both sides of me as I sat there with my head against the wall. Sometimes it took a couple hours, but eventually the two of them became so worn out that they'd just decide to go to sleep. After all these years, it felt like nothing had changed.

As the weeks went on, it felt like I had lost the ability to think clearly. More than ever before, depression and intrusive thoughts consumed me. Every fear and every negative thought that my mind could conjure up played itself on repeat every hour of every day. I prayed often, but especially when I felt my mental state was at its worst. When the nagging voice in my head dared me to jump in front of a car, or wait for the train that passed by my high school.

Each day, I spent the forty-five-minute walk to and from school contending with the negative thoughts and anxiety that overwhelmed me. In these moments, I tried to focus my mind, just for a moment, on saying something to God. But my prayer for help was almost always interrupted by the negative thoughts. Most prayers went unfinished because it felt like my mind wouldn't let me.

Mom and Ron still attended drug and alcohol meetings several times a week, and, although I didn't understand why at first, I started going with them, and I enjoyed it. I sat around a crackling fire, watching embers float into the sky as I listened to men and women of all ages and backgrounds share stories about their past.

I was captivated by their stories of hardship and how they rose up and made the choice to change their lives. I wondered what motivated them and what kept them going. But perhaps what I was really seeking were the testimonies of those who learned about Jesus and His love along the way. How in the midst of all their disaster, He picked them up out of their brokenness and loved them without judgement of who they once were. This was why I went.

Three nights a week, I sat around a bonfire or in an old garage, listening to these stories that gave me hope.

I didn't share my interest in God with anyone. I was still trying to figure it out on my own. However, Mom had recently started praying and attending Bible studies. She said that God was the reason she lived long enough to get sober and have her kids back in her life. She said she owed everything to Him. It was an adjustment hearing her speak this way, so lovingly and sensitively, but I knew she was sincere. As she shared these thoughts, I listened quietly, pretending to have no real interest but desperately wanting to hear more.

Chapter 28

Another year passed. It was 2006 and by this time, it had been over three years since Todd was arrested, but even with the recorded confession, Todd hadn't been convicted and I was still attending court dates. Each time another hearing was scheduled, I mentally prepared for walking into the courtroom and looking at Todd while reliving the details of his abuse.

Over the year I struggled, sometimes more than I thought I could handle. There was a constant war within my mind, like something was fighting against me. Prayer became the one thing I clung to because it was the only thing that gave me any relief.

I had thought that becoming a Christian meant I'd suddenly be set free from all the things that tormented me. I thought that once I had experienced the presence of God, everything else would have to leave me alone. But I learned that that wasn't how it worked, at least for me. Perhaps this hellish place my mind was in was a result of everything I had seen, heard, and experienced all the years leading up to this point. Healing would be a process.

Chapter 29

With my eighteenth birthday two months away, I planned to move in with Jay. He had told me over the months how he couldn't wait for us to start our life together. Although we still had our arguments at times, things were better between us. Once work calmed down for him, we began seeing each other and talking regularly again, which helped my peace of mind. And even though he still questioned me from time to time, we had far more good days than bad.

As it got closer to my birthday I dreaded the conversation with my mother that I would be moving out, and I wondered how I'd explain my relationship with Jay to her. I played scenarios in my head over and over until I got tired. I didn't want to hurt her or make her feel like I was moving out to get away from her. And I never wanted to make her feel as if I resented her for the past because I didn't. But Mom and I didn't share a close relationship, and although she tried in her own ways, I was incapable of letting my guard down. I didn't share my worries or concerns with her, or even say I love you, unless I felt obligated to say it back. Our relationship was complex, but I loved her very much. I felt moving out was best for me, and it would also allow me to build a relationship with her at my own pace.

About three days before my birthday, I told my mother that I was going to stay with some friends. Really I was going to stay with Jay.

"Well, you're eighteen now, and you can do whatever you want," she said softly.

Her voice was sad.

"Well, I guess so, but that's not what this is about," I said kindly.

She paused and looked at me. Her eyes squinted in the sunlight coming from the window. The past two years had come and gone. In this moment, I sensed that she prayed she did everything she could to be a good mother and to make up for her past. I knew she was haunted by the things she had done, and that her depression was as deep as mine, perhaps much deeper. I thought about this often, and it pained me. I knew she'd take back every hurtful thing she ever did if she could. And I wished that she could, not for my own sake, but for hers. I wanted her to be free from the guilt she lived with.

She lingered as if she had something more to say.

"Okay, well go have fun," she said finally.

"Thank you, Mom."

"Text me so I know you're safe!" she shouted as I headed down the hall.

After all this time waiting, I was finally eighteen. Within the hour, I had a bag packed and was on my way to see Jay.

The next couple of days I spent going to dinners and celebrating with Jay. For the first time in a long time, I felt truly happy. By the end of the night, I had a voicemail from my mother.

"Hey, Jess. I don't expect you to call me back. I know you're probably busy having a good time, but I wanted to tell you that I love you. Happy birthday, my daughter."

The next morning, I called my mom. I had dreaded this moment, but it was time to be honest with her.

"It's okay. You've got this," Jay said as I reached for the phone.

He sat anxiously on the edge of the bed, waiting as I paced the room.

"Your Mom has come a long way. I bet she'll be happy for you and us." His words were reassuring.

"Okay."

I looked down at the phone and dialed, and before the phone could finish the first ring, she picked up.

"Hey, Jess!"

"Hey, Mom. How's it goin' at home?"

"Good! Just been workin' on the yard. Those rose bushes weren't lookin' so good. How was yesterday?"

"It was good, I had a nice dinner at an old Italian restaurant. Then we saw a movie."

"Oh that sounds nice, Jess."

"Actually, Mom, there's somethin' I wanted to talk to you about."

There was a long pause on the other end.

"Okay."

"Do you remember Jay? You met him a few years ago? He knew Todd and Derek."

She hesitated. "Yes."

"Well, that's who I'm with right now."

I stood frozen, peering at the carpet. There was silence.

Finally, she laughed. "No way!"

"Yeah, he's here right now."

"Jay? You two are seeing each other now?"

"Yes."

Again there was silence.

"Well, Jess, I'm happy for you, darlin'. If he makes you happy, then I'm happy."

By her tone, I didn't exactly believe her, but I knew I needed to give her time to process all of this.

"He does make me happy. I'm glad you're okay with this."

"Of course, Jess. Well, I gotta run to the store, but call me later, okay?"

"Okay, Mom. Will do."

I let out a heavy sigh. The weight I had felt for so long began to lift off of me. Jay stood up to give me a hug.

"You did it! Now we really can start our lives together."

Chapter 30

The first few weeks that Jay and I lived together were great. We loved seeing each other every day, and we did everything together. Patricia, Jay's mother, moved in with him shortly before I did. Because of her declining health, he wanted her close. But she and I had formed a great relationship. She loved me and even called me her daughter.

However, things became more stressful for us when, within a couple of months, Jay was only going to work a couple days a week. Soon, he wasn't bringing in enough money to pay the rent or any of the bills. Eventually, he stopped working entirely. At the same time, he began staying up late at night, sometimes all night. It seemed like he was just letting his business go, and I couldn't understand until one morning when I was doing laundry.

I stood over the washer, throwing in clothes. I reached inside the pocket of Jay's jeans, and I couldn't believe what I found: drugs. It was a small sealed bag with a white substance inside. I grew up finding bags like this that my parents left lying around.

I felt disgusted. I didn't want to believe that Jay was using drugs, but as I thought about it, it explained a lot. Later that evening, when Jay returned home, I was waiting for him in the bedroom.

"Hey, baby!" he said happily as he walked in.

"Hi." I normally got up for a kiss, but this time I didn't.
"Everything okay?" he asked.
"No," I said, disappointed.
I got up and handed him the bag I found in his pocket.
"Are you snooping through my stuff?"
"I found it when I was doing your laundry," I snapped back.
"Throw it away. I don't care. I knew it was a mistake anyway."
"We're not those kind of people, Jay. We don't do things like this."
"I know. I said throw it away!"

Jay didn't like being questioned, ever, about anything. He said it was a trigger for him and made him feel like he was back in custody being interrogated. This made me nervous to ask him things, and when I did, I had to ask myself if it were even worth it. It didn't feel fair to never be allowed to communicate or ask questions about anything, but his temper scared me.

Weeks went by, and Jay still wasn't working. He began selling some of his extra equipment to pay the bills, but the money he made still wasn't enough, and rent was always late. Several more weeks went by, and he began listing some of his vehicles and work trucks for sale.

The money he got never lasted us long. He said it was going toward paying off debts and his mother's medical bills. Jay had gone from having more money than he knew what to do with to not having enough to pay our electricity or gas bill. Things were declining fast, and soon I was taking cold showers each night because we didn't have hot water. At times, I even wished I was back home with my mother.

I loved Jay, but he didn't seem to mind the bills paid late or the cold showers. I asked him what was going on, what was keeping him from looking for work. He told me he'd been experiencing depression. This was no surprise to me as he had shared with me in the past that the thought of his daughter often put him in a depressive state of mind.

At the same time, I started to see more of his temper again. But I was so used to people in my life losing their temper every once in a while, that as much as I didn't like it, this didn't seem like something to be too concerned about. Although, Jay seemed to lose his temper more regularly as time went on.

One evening, I walked through the front door to see Jay standing in the living room. It looked like he was waiting for me.

"What took you so long to get home today?" he asked.

I stopped in my tracks. "I told you I was going to my mom's after work."

The dark circles under his eyes told me he hadn't been sleeping much, and his jaw clenched tightly as I spoke.

"You're a liar. You didn't tell me that."

I looked at him, confused.

"I did tell you that."

Jay didn't respond to me. Instead, he took two steps to the right and reached for a small speaker that was sitting next to the TV. With the speaker gripped in his hand, he drew back his arm and threw it at me. It sliced open the skin of my calf.

"What's wrong with you?" I cried.

But he didn't say a word. Instead, he turned and left the room. Blood dripped down to my ankle. I stepped into the kitchen for a paper towel, then sat on the couch, carefully cleaning myself up.

I stayed away from Jay for the next couple of hours until later that evening, I confronted him about what happened. He accused me of provoking that kind of behavior from him. "You could've answered me simply, but instead you gave me attitude. That's why you got hurt."

I thought about what he said. I did have an attitude. Mom always told me that. I supposed he was right.

Chapter 31

It had been several months that I lived with Jay, and I still had some things in boxes. So one afternoon, while Jay was gone, I decided to organize the closets in our bedroom. I turned the radio on, pulled the blinds up to let the sunshine in, and pulled back the closet door. I sat on the carpet, moving pairs of shoes and old boxes filled with paperwork. I gushed over sweet old pictures of him and his sister when they were kids. There were moments when everything just felt all right, and this was one of them.

After another thirty minutes had passed, it was time to wrap it up and be done. I picked up those old boxes of paperwork and old invoices and placed them on the left side of the closet. This would now be Jay's side. As I lifted the boxes to stack them, a tattered handwritten note stuck to the bottom of a box caught my attention. I grabbed it and put the boxes down. Before I could unfold the letter, I saw what was written at the bottom of the page.

"I Love You. - Danielle"

It felt like my heart stopped beating. My eyes wandered up to the top of the page and began reading.

"You make me happier than I've ever been. I'm so in love with you ..."

I couldn't move.

"I can't wait to see you this weekend."

The words were blurred through my tears. Even with the radio, the room felt silent. The letter was dated during the time that Jay had stopped visiting me. He always said it was because of work, even on the weekends.

My body slouched, and the paper slowly slipped through my fingers onto the carpet. I was devastated. I suddenly felt broken, and I didn't know if I'd ever feel whole again. I leaned back and lay on the floor with the letter next to me. Eventually, the carpet beneath me was soaked with the tears that had fallen from my face.

But suddenly, I felt a gentle exchange of grief for anger. I got off the floor and walked outside to the front porch to wait for Jay's truck to pull up. Hours passed. I paced the house and the front porch; I couldn't keep still. My mind raced and I questioned everything I thought I knew. Soon, I was exhausted. I took a shower and then lay in bed. At last, I heard the front door open and his voice come down the hall. The bedroom door opened, and he stopped in his tracks as soon as he looked at me.

"What's wrong?" he asked, worried.

I held up the letter. He stared back at me without saying a word. Then he tried to explain himself, but none of it mattered. He explained that for a brief time he and Danielle were seeing each other. He said that he thought I was involved with someone else and that he was devastated. He said this was the only reason he did what he did. I didn't believe any of it. I cried for hours. In the days following, I slept as much as I could. When I wasn't asleep, I walked around in a fog.

I spent the next week speaking to Jay as little as possible and sleeping as much as I could. Until, eventually, I chose to forgive him.

I had never had anyone I could count on or that loved me. Jay had been the only one, and I had grown to need him more than I needed to be respected and valued. The girl that was raised to be tough and not need anyone or anything now needed love so much that she was willing to be mistreated, abused, and cheated on by a man and still not leave. I hated that about myself.

Chapter 32

Before the summer was over, I attended the last court date in my case against Todd. It had been nearly four years since I handed over his confession. I had been to countless court dates and sat in front of a courtroom of strangers, sharing details of some of the most embarrassing moments I could recall. I had dealt with severe anxiety each time I entered the courtroom, followed by ruthless guilt when I walked out. For years, he was my father, and now he sat in front of me in a prison jumpsuit with tears streaming down his face. For brief moments, those tears made me question if it was all worth it. I wasn't just ruining *his* life, I was taking away Paul's father, who he loved very much.

But I knew that it *was* worth it. I knew that Todd had never once considered the destructive path he was putting his five-year-old daughter on. Or how each day she'd become more broken and more insecure.

I stepped into the courtroom for the last time. My body trembled with nervousness, but I took a deep breath and held my head high. I approached the stand where I'd raise my right hand for the last time.

"Do you swear to tell the truth, the whole truth, and nothing but the truth so help you God?"

"Yes."

"Please be seated."

I looked out at my mother and Jay in the audience. They looked at me calm and confident. I could feel Todd's eyes watching me, but I decided I wouldn't look back at him until I wanted to. I kept my gaze on the attorney. I could see Todd moving from side to side and back and forth. He tapped on the desk in front of him and sighed loudly. He was desperate for me to look at him.

To my left were pictures of me of when I was a child. They were pinned to a poster board. There was a picture of me smiling from ear to ear. Mom would say that my eyes were like little moons in this photo. I was in a bathtub full of bubbles. In my hand was one of my favorite dolls. I was holding up her knitted blue dress to give her a bath. I had to explain that when that picture of me was taken, I was already being molested by my father. I could hear the faint crying of my mother in the audience as I spoke. Another three pictures were pointed to, and I was asked to give details of what I could remember at that time. As I spoke, I wished that my mother wasn't in the room. I didn't want her to hear these things.

It felt like I had been on the stand for longer than I ever had. My neck and shoulders were sore from being so tense. I felt exhausted.

Finally, the attorney stepped aside, and there was a brief break in the questioning. I turned my head slightly to the left and looked Todd in the eyes. I could see the vein in his forehead as he glared back at me. Looking into his eyes, I knew he hated me. I held my gaze.

Minutes later, the attorney returned, and the questioning continued. Finally, after spending several hours at the courthouse, I was dismissed, and I left the stand, knowing I'd never have to go back.

Todd was found guilty and sentenced to sixteen years in prison.

Two months later, Jay and I had to move out of our house. All the money was gone, and we had an eviction notice on the door. With Patricia's help, we were able to get a place to stay in Antioch, about an hour from Patterson. Steve and Carol had been good friends of Patricia's for years, and once they heard about our situation, they offered to help. They had a large two-story home with three empty bedrooms. They offered to let us rent one of them until Jay was able to find us our own place and get back to work.

Within two weeks, we were moved out of Patterson and living in Antioch. We moved in with just a small amount of clothes and a TV. Everything else was sold or left behind in a storage unit. I applied for a hostess job at the café down the road and was hired almost immediately. I was grateful to get a job so quickly.

It didn't take long before there was tension in the house. Steve and Carol had started to see Jay's short fuse and cocky attitude, and they didn't want him around much longer. They told him he had two weeks to find us another place. In private, they pulled me aside and apologized. They said it had nothing to do with me and that they were sorry, but we had to go. I didn't blame them. Jay had been walking around the house like it was his own.

Two weeks passed, and Jay confronted Steve downstairs in the living room. This was the day we were supposed to be moving out, but instead, Jay told Steve he refused to move out and that he'd stay as long as he liked. Within days, Steve served Jay with an eviction notice.

With nowhere else to go, we checked into a motel for the next couple of nights. Jay still wasn't looking for work, and had it not been for my job at the café, we wouldn't have been able to afford to do this.

Three months later, I was promoted to a server. I took as many shifts as they'd give me, and I picked up as many extra tables up as I could. It seemed like every dollar I was making was going toward just surviving. We were still staying at the motel. Although I had found an apartment, I needed to save up for the deposit. Even with all of the extra shifts I was working, we were barely making it.

I kept all of this from my mother—and everyone. I was embarrassed by the situation I suddenly found myself in. I couldn't understand how things went from good to bad so quickly. I felt lost.

Chapter 33

It was late one afternoon, and I had just gotten home from a long day at work. My feet were sore, and I planned to rest for a few minutes before heading to the store for dinner. My phone rang but not knowing the number, I ignored it. One minute later, I had a voicemail.

"Jesse, this is Rosemary, your dad's sister." Her voice sounded raspy and low. "I've got some news to tell you … Please call me back, honey."

I didn't know Rosemary. I had only heard about her. I called her back right away.

"Rosemary, it's Jessica. I got your voicemail."

"Oh, honey, I'm so sorry." Her voice began to crack. "I hate to be the one to tell you this, but your dad passed away last night."

I replayed her words in my head until they made sense.

"How?"

"He died in his sleep, honey. He went peacefully."

She said that the night before he had gone on a date, the first date he had been on in years. When he got home, he smiled as he told his roommates all about her and that they were going to see each other again the following weekend. He said goodnight and walked out of the back door to the yard, where he lived in an in-law unit. The next morning, his roommate got up and saw

John's truck still parked outside. John was usually gone early for work so he went to his door and knocked. He knocked again and called his name, but nothing happened. He opened up his door to see him lying in his bed. Next to him, on a small table, was an old silver spoon and a lighter.

John was fifty-four years old, and he had used heroin for decades. I knew his body must've been tired from a life like that. But there were still so many questions I had for him.

Later that week, I drove to his house in Martinez. I wanted to get something, anything, to remember him by. I arrived and was greeted at the door by John's roommates. They led me through the kitchen to the back door.

"Alright, well, he didn't have much, but take whatever you want."

I walked down the steps and up to his door. I paused for a moment to take a deep breath, then I walked in. It was dark; the shades kept all sunlight from shining through. The air was stale, and the floor was littered with tools, old papers, and clothes.

I carefully stepped over beer cans and old jeans and walked over to a small cabinet, hoping to find something I could take home with me. Inside was an old photo album. I opened it up and saw pictures of him when he was a child with grandparents I had never met. I closed the photo album, then took a long look at his room and the way he lived. I then headed toward the door. I grabbed his old pair of sunglasses before leaving.

It was too bad the time we spent together ended in disaster, but at least I could laugh about it now. And to be fair, there were times he tried to be a good father. Once, while I was in foster care, he drove all the way to Modesto to bring me a coat. He had known through a letter I wrote to him that I didn't have one and that the weather had been cold. The following week he took the hour and a half drive to meet me after school and give me the beautiful fur coat he bought me. It was light brown with soft white fur; it was the nicest coat I had ever owned. He said hello to me, handed me the coat, and then said goodbye. I knew he was nervous and just didn't know how to talk to me.

Another time he sent me a small check with a shaky handwritten note, and at the end, he wrote, "Love, Dad." It's something I still have tucked away in an old shoe box in my closet.

Chapter 34

It took many long hours, but I managed to get enough money saved for a deposit. I applied for an apartment at Cross Pointe. It was a great location; I could walk across the street to the small grocery store or the coffee shop on the corner. I was excited to have a place to call home. I knew there'd be even more pressure on me to work long hours, but it was all worth it.

Despite Jay not working and making life harder than it needed to be sometimes, I was still moving forward, and I felt good about that. And after all the months of my mother asking to come see where I was living, I could finally invite her over. Things were falling into place, sort of.

But shortly after moving into the apartment, it felt like the good days were few and far between. Some days Jay was the most loving guy. He wrote me letters telling me that I was the only one that's ever really loved him and that he didn't know how he could ever live without me. These were the things I lived for, and I soaked up every word. But then there were days that I would come home from a long day at work to find him upset and waiting to argue with me about something. He would question me repeatedly about things as if he didn't trust me at all.

Because I was the only one working and all of my money was going to bills, there wasn't much money to be spent on groceries. I had to shop smart, and I couldn't afford to buy a lot at one time. But Jay would get mad that I wasn't keeping more food in the house. Or he'd be upset that he'd finish the dinner I made for him, and he'd still be hungry; sometimes I was still hungry too. Still, Jay refused to get a job himself. He said that after owning his own successful business, he wasn't ever going to work a low paying nine-to-five, no matter how badly we needed the money. He promised that eventually he was going to start up his construction business again.

In the evenings, Jay would go down to the garage, then not come back up for hours. Eventually, he began to stay out there all night, and sometimes when I woke up in the morning, he'd still be out there. I asked him why he wasn't sleeping. He'd tell me that it was insomnia and depression, and he thanked me for being so understanding. When I asked him to see someone for help, he said he wouldn't.

I believed him that it was insomnia and depression, but after this continued for several more weeks, I felt that the only explanation for this was that Jay had to be using drugs to keep him awake. So I decided to confront him about it. But when I did, he denied it and became so upset with me that I regretted saying anything at all. Then he accused *me* of hiding something.

However, about one week after he denied using drugs, I found some in the pocket of his jeans. My heart sank, and I felt disgusted. I couldn't bear the thought of it. I paced the apartment, looking for the right way to talk to him about it when he got home. I wanted so badly to believe this wasn't a regular thing for him. The times in the past that I suspected that he was using, he would deny it. Then later that night, he'd sleep a solid eight to ten hours. After a couple of times, I came to not trust my own judgment. All the years Mom and Todd were using, they never slept. I concluded that I was being paranoid and that I didn't know what I was talking about anymore.

One day while at work, a coworker told me about the church he attended and how they had a Bible study group that met in Concord each week. He told me there were a lot of great people there, and that I should check it out. I had never attended a Bible study, and I had only attended a church a few times in my life so I was excited to go. When I got home later that day, I asked Jay if he'd come with me, and to my surprise, he agreed.

Later that week, we went, and I loved it. I loved the soft sound of the guitar playing as we all sang together, and I loved that people I didn't know came up to me, gently placed their hands on my shoulder, and prayed for me. I felt encouraged, and it made me feel like all of the chaos around me suddenly didn't matter.

So, I decided to go back. But after the second visit, Jay told me that he wouldn't attend anymore. He said he didn't like the people and that he especially didn't like the guy who led the group, the youth pastor, Javier. He insisted that he had a thing for me. But Javier and I had hardly even spoke to one another. I ignored Jay and continued to attend each Thursday night for the next several weeks until Jay forbade me from going back. He said he had a "bad feeling" about the youth pastor, and he accused me of having a thing for him. When I denied it, he put me through intense questioning about it that lasted for several hours. Rather than fighting it any longer, I gave up and decided I wouldn't attend anymore.

So I stopped going, and instead I decided I'd attend the church service they had on Sunday mornings. Jay told me that I could only go if he went with me, but I wanted him to go anyway. I thought, whether he wanted it to or not, it would help him.

Several weeks went by, and Jay decided that he'd no longer attend church with me so I continued to go by myself. I loved it so much that I didn't mind going alone; it was what I looked forward to all week. I also started reading my Bible every day. It encouraged me and gave me a new sense of hope.

Chapter 35

Jay insisted that I couldn't trust anyone, and because of that, it was for my own good that I didn't talk about anything personal and that I didn't make friends at the cafe. For several weeks, I kept it a secret that I had made two close friends at work, Monica and Amy. The three of us were all nineteen, and I felt like I was building authentic friendships, which was something I had never really had before. Finally, as time went on and our friendship became more cherished, I decided to tell Jay about them.

When I did, he became angry, and he insisted that I never listened to him. Jay was constantly warning me about people, even my own mom and brother, saying he was trying to protect me from people that would betray me. But I started to feel that he was worried I'd open up to someone about how he was treating me. Jay wasn't trying to protect me; he was trying to isolate me from people that *could* help me.

Before leaving for work in the mornings, I got the brunt of Jay's anger. I was emotionally spent from his constant questioning. Soon, I wasn't even finding reprieve when I was at work because he started showing up at the cafe during my shifts. He would come in, say hi to me, and then leave. I knew he was checking up on me, and sometimes he even told me that.

As the weeks passed, sometimes Jay would show up to my work but he wouldn't even come into the building. Instead, I'd see his truck parked outside or a coworker would tell me that they saw him sitting on the patio. When I'd look for him, he'd be gone. Later, when I'd arrive home after work, he'd be waiting at the table for me with a series of questions, like who did I talk to that day and who was that guy standing next to me by the computer. He said that through the window of the restaurant, he could see me having a conversation with a guy. The guy was a coworker, but that didn't matter; I was told to never talk to him again, and if I did, he would find out.

It felt like Jay's anger and paranoia were getting out of control. I began paying closer attention to what I did throughout the day so I could have an answer for Jay later on when he asked. I would learn that tiny details of my day that I never paid attention to were now the things that Jay would question me about. And the times I couldn't recall the details of what he was asking, he'd interrogate me, sometimes threatening to hit me until I gave him an answer. This was torturous and would, at times, go on for hours.

Jay suffered from lower back pain so, a couple times a week, we'd go sit in the hot tub downstairs in our apartment complex so he could get some relief. One evening, Jay sat across from me and didn't speak to me. Just from the look on his face, I could see he was bothered. But I knew well enough to stay quiet when he was like this. I didn't know why Jay was mad, but Jay didn't need a reason. By this time, I had spent so much mental energy trying to deduce why Jay did this or that, I had come to terms with there usually not being a reason why Jay was behaving the way that he was. So I sat quietly in the hot tub while he ignored me.

After about fifteen minutes, he wanted to leave. I stepped out of the water, wrapped my towel around me, and began leaving the pool area. We walked out of the pool gate, then started walking the small, winding path back to the apartment.

"You know I hate that swimsuit," he remarked.

I turned around to look at him. Not knowing what to say, I turned back around.

"It makes you look like a whore."

My eyes welled with tears. I stopped again and looked back at him.

"Why do you have to be so mean?" I asked him.

He looked back at me without saying anything. I turned back around and continued walking as tears fell down my face.

Suddenly, I felt the force of Jay's hands on my back as he shoved me down to the ground. I fell hard. My right hand fell in the shrubs, and my left on the concrete. I remained there on my hands and knees in shock for a moment. I could feel the stinging of my knee, and the pathway beneath me became blurry through the tears in my eyes. Moments later, Jay walked past me and continued on to our apartment as I was hunched over on the ground. I took a moment, then I slowly I got up. My left knee bled and so did the palm of my hand. I picked the small rocks and dirt out of my right hand, and stood up. I grabbed my towel off of the ground, then looked to see if there were anyone around. I hoped that no one saw what happened.

When I opened the apartment door and stepped inside, Jay acted as if nothing happened. He leaned back on the couch and turned on the TV. I walked past him timidly and entered the bedroom. I took a long hot shower, then I went to sleep.

The next day, Jay transformed back into a loving, compassionate person again. He told me he realized how mean he was acting toward me and that he was sorry. He reminded me that the anger he experienced at times was a result of so many years of being mistreated in prison and how this was not his fault. I felt that if I loved Jay, I needed to love him unconditionally and I needed to be that loyal person that I was always told to be. I needed to be there and help Jay because I was all he had.

"I hate that I get like that. It's just that after so many years in prison, it changes a person. Just know that I love you and that I see how patient you are with me," Jay explained.

"You're so mean sometimes, and I hate it." I said tearfully.

"I know, and I'm so sorry. This anger isn't about you, and I'm sorry I take it out on you. You're the one person in this world who hasn't given up on me."

His words rang in my ears. I was the only person who hadn't given up on him.

I knew I shouldn't forgive so easily, but I did. He held me in his arms, and I cried quietly. Perhaps, I hoped, that us talking about this was the turning point where things would get better.

Chapter 36

For the couple of weeks following our discussion, we were happy. I would come home to sweet notes and little surprises. Jay was returning to the man he used to be.

Many times over the past several of years, Jay had brought up marriage. However, being as young as I was, I went back and forth about the idea. But Jay had a beautiful diamond ring made for me. After I turned eighteen, he gave it to me.

I accepted the ring knowing that we would get married one day. However, after all our problems, it seemed less and less likely that either of us were desiring marriage. There just never seemed to be a right time.

Yet, as Jay began to make amends for his behavior, I threw aside all common sense in exchange to feel happy again. Jay asked me to marry him, and I said yes. We planned to get married at the Martinez courthouse the following week.

In the days leading up to the ceremony, I thought of what our future would look like, whether we would have kids, but it was hard to see any of that. I also couldn't see ever living without Jay either, and the thought of it scared me. As much as prayer had become so important to me, I never once bothered praying about whether I should marry Jay or not. Perhaps deep down, I was scared God would tell me I shouldn't. And at that time in my life, it was what I wanted so that's all that mattered to me.

Finally, it was the big day. I remember getting up that morning and I remember the drive to Martinez. Monica drove us, Amy was with her. The two of them were as loving and supportive as they could possibly be that day, although I wonder now how they really felt about what I was doing.

After arriving at the courthouse, I have no recollection of getting married. What I do remember is what took place after arriving back to the apartment. While ignoring me, Jay walked into our bedroom angry, changed his clothes, and went to bed. Within minutes, he was asleep.

I sat alone at the kitchen table in my white dress, hating myself for what I had done. Being married wasn't supposed to feel this way.

An hour had passed, and I decided I'd let Jay sleep, hoping that he'd wake up in a better mood. I decided that I'd start preparing dinner so when he woke up it would be ready for him. Then I hoped we would watch a movie or do something fun together.

But another hour went by, and Jay was still asleep. I became impatient and went into the room to wake him up.

"What?" he shouted. "Why are you waking me up?"

My eyes filled with tears.

"Today's our wedding day. Don't you want to spend time together?"

He let out a deep sigh of frustration and sat up.

"You just can't let me sleep, can you?" he shouted.

I quickly retreated back to the kitchen table and regretted my choice to wake him up. He walked into the kitchen after me and opened the fridge for a drink. He slammed the refrigerator door shut and then made his way back to the bed.

"Don't wake me up again!" he yelled as he walked past me.

Within minutes, I could hear him sleeping again. I had never felt lonelier. Hours passed, and I couldn't bring myself to get up out of the chair. This behavior would continue for the next several days, and eventually I'd realize that the nice Jay was gone once again. He was here just long enough for me to marry him.

Chapter 37

Around this time, an old friend in Merced had a litter of puppies she was looking for homes for. Desperate for something to curb the loneliness and depression I felt, I decided to get one. One week later, I took the trip to pick mine up.

There were two girls and a boy. I chose the boy. As soon as I lay eyes on him, I was in love. He had auburn fur with a small white stripe between his eyes and the roundest belly. He was exactly what I needed, and I couldn't have been happier. I named him Bruce.

Jay and I had been married for only one month when I came home from work to experience the worst beating I had ever gotten from him. When I arrived home, he was sitting on the couch. He wasn't watching TV; instead, he was waiting for me. We looked at each other, and he flashed me an evil-looking smirk.

"Come with me. I have something to show you," he said calmly.

I sighed. I was tired from working all day, and the heels of my feet were throbbing, begging me to sit down.

I walked into the bedroom, took my apron and shoes off, and threw them on the floor. I sat on the bed for a moment and mentally prepared for another agonizing conversation with Jay. I gathered up all the strength I had and stood. I changed my clothes, then walked back into the living room.

"Great. Let's go for a walk," he said, smiling and sarcastic.

We walked outside, and the apartment door slammed behind us.

"You're in for a surprise!" he told me as he looked back with a large grin on his face.

I became aggravated quickly, but I knew better than to show it right then. We walked out of the apartment complex and across the street. I became curious where we could possibly be going.

"Are you ready for this?" He turned around and asked, "I bet you had no idea I'd find out, did you?"

I wanted to scream. I had no idea what he was talking about. He looked back at me periodically and smiled as he led the way. We then entered another apartment complex across the street.

"Okay. I give up. Where are we going?" I asked, annoyed.

He stopped and looked back at me.

"Well, where do you think?"

"I have no idea Jay."

He laughed. "The cop. You know, the one you're sleepin' with. This is his apartment."

"What? Have you lost your mind?"

"You didn't think I'd find out, but I did."

"I'm not even gonna argue with you; this is absolutely crazy."

He laughed again and then pointed up to the window where he believed the man I was supposedly sleeping with lived. Jay scrutinized everything I did and said. And even though I was innocent of what he was accusing me of, I was terrified I would in some way act suspicious or in a way that made him think I was lying. I kept asking myself, *Do I get mad? Or do I simply not react at all? What is it that Jay expects me to do?* But it didn't matter what I did because Jay would find fault in any way I chose to react.

We started the walk back to our apartment. We didn't speak to one another; I didn't know what I could even say to him. He had lost his mind, and there was no point in trying to argue with him. We made our way up our stairs, and he unlocked the front door.

"Come in," he said with a smile.

I had a horrible feeling in the pit of my stomach. Frightened, I walked in slowly as I kept my eyes on him. The sound of the door shutting behind me sounded more like a metal prison door locking me inside a cell. I wasn't ready for what was going to happen next.

He walked past me and turned the lock on the door. Then, suddenly, before I even knew what was happening, his fist came toward my face. He gripped my hair with one hand and began punching the side of my face with the other.

"You whore!" he said as he hit me. I reached up with both my hands to try to block my face and relieve the pressure from him pulling my hair. He threw me to the ground and then picked me up again, only to throw me back down even harder.

I lay on the floor, disoriented, while my head throbbed just as hard as my chest.

"You think you can lie to me and I won't find out?"

"I've never lied to you," I said from the floor. "Please believe me."

He picked me up once again. This time he lifted my whole body up off the ground, and then he threw me into the wall. My body fell down onto the floor, leaving broken sheetrock above me.

"Don't you say a word!" he said to me.

Terrified, I kept silent.

White powder from the cracked sheetrock was on my clothing. I lay on the ground, praying he was done, and I tried to catch my breath. Within seconds, he was standing in front of me once again. With both hands, he gripped the back of my shirt and lifted me up off the ground.

"Please, stop. I promise you I'm not lying!" Nothing I said was helping me.

He threw me back down onto the floor. He bent down and then flipped me over onto my stomach; then he got on top of me. He placed his knee in the center of my back and pressed down with all of his weight. Next, he pressed my head down into the floor as hard as he could. The pressure was too much to take. I screamed as loud as I could and prayed that the neighbors beneath us would hear me and come help.

Jay quickly flipped me over onto my back and gripped my hair. Spit came from his mouth as he held his hand over my mouth and told me to shut up.

Then, as he sat on my chest, he repeatedly punched both sides of my head. I could feel my brain being rocked from side to side. I cannot recall the next few minutes. What I do remember next is the downstairs neighbors banging on their ceiling and yelling at us to be quiet. Then Jay abruptly got off of me and walked to the bedroom. After some time had gone by, I crawled over to the couch and cried myself to sleep.

For the next three nights, I slept on the couch. I didn't speak to Jay, and he hardly spoke to me. He walked around the house casually with a carelessness about him. He enjoyed seeing me in pain, but more than anything, he enjoyed being feared, a disposition I was all too familiar with.

Chapter 38

Over the next few weeks, as I'd take Bruce for his walks, there was a woman that I would run into often. Her name was Kathy, and she lived in the same building as me.

I thought she was beautiful. She had pretty blonde hair and a big smile. I'd always see her out walking her dog, and each time we ran into each other, she'd smile and say hello to me.

"How are you, dear?" she'd ask.

I'd make small talk and avoid talking about what was really going on in my life.

"Well, if you ever need anything, knock on my door," she'd say.

She was kind, and I knew she was sincere. Over time, she began to tell me that she was praying for me, and she always reminded me that I could come to her apartment if I ever were in trouble. I always wondered what made her say those things to me. I politely thanked her, but I never told her what was really going on.

Until one day, a couple weeks later, I showed up at her door. I had come home from work to find Jay in an antagonistic state of mind that I thought would lead to him hitting me. He started by questioning me about why it took me so long to walk home. When he walked into the other room, I quickly left. Seconds later, I was knocking at Kathy's door.

"Come in, honey," she said as soon as she saw me standing there.

"I'm sorry, but I needed a safe place to hang out for a little while."

"It's okay, honey. Tell me what happened."

I wasn't sure why, but I felt like I could trust her. So, for the first time, I told someone that Jay was hitting me. She wasn't surprised.

"I've always known something was going on. That's why I always told you to come here if you needed help."

We sat at her kitchen table as her radio played Christian music in the background.

"Honey, years ago, I was with a man who beat me. It was easy for me to see the signs with you."

"Well, I thought it would stop."

"They never stop," she said to me with conviction.

This wasn't something I wanted to accept.

"You need to figure out what you're going to do, honey, because it will only get worse the longer you stay."

I thought about what she said. I believed her, but my heart was still holding on to hope that this would all stop.

I left an hour later and walked back to my apartment, and I continued to think about what Kathy said to me.

"Where the hell have you been?" Jay asked as I walked in the front door.

I knew I had to be honest.

"I went to Kathy's house. I knew you were in a bad mood, and I didn't feel safe here."

"Oh, shut up! You act like I beat you," he snapped back.

"You do."

He laughed. "If I wanted to beat you, I would. I could hurt you real bad if I wanted to, but I don't 'cause I don't beat women."

It was true that he could hurt me badly if he wanted to. Was he right? Was this not really as bad as I thought? I no longer knew what to believe. But two weeks later, I was knocking on Kathy's door again.

"I'm sorry to show up again. I came home from work, and he started throwing things at me. He said he saw me talking to a guy at work."

"Don't apologize. You can come here whenever you need to. Now, how did he know who you were talking to at work?"

"He came to the restaurant. He said that he'd been watching me from outside and that I was talking to one of the guys I work with."

"Oh my goodness!" She sighed.

"Now he thinks I have something going on with my coworker, but I talk to everyone I work with."

"This is crazy, honey. You can't stay there much longer."

Just then, from the kitchen table, I saw Jay walk by.

"Oh no! Here he comes!"

"Go hide in the bedroom," she whispered.

Frantic, I ran into her bedroom and then behind her bathroom door. Jay knocked on the door.

"Hi," Kathy answered. Her tone was upbeat and friendly as if she had no idea why he was there.

"Is Jess over here?"

"Nope. I haven't seen her yet today. Is everything okay?"

"Yeah. She left a little while ago and I don't know where she went. That's all."

"Oh, okay. Well, I'll let ya know if I see her."

Then I heard the door close. *Thank God,* I thought. She closed the blinds, and I spent the rest of the evening in Kathy's apartment. I knew this meant I'd have to come up with a good excuse for where I was, but at that point, I didn't care.

As time went on, things continued to get worse. My mom and Paul still didn't know anything that was happening, and any phone calls from them had gone unanswered pretty consistently. I would text them and tell them that I was working, even if I wasn't. It was always pride that kept me from telling them what was going on; I was ashamed that I had let myself get into an abusive relationship. But now I was too scared of what Jay would do if he found out I told them.

Work became a place I loved and hated. It was my refuge from the chaos and terror that waited for me at home. But it also became another prison. Because Jay knew where to find me. Sometimes he would walk in and then walk out simply so I would know he was there, watching me. Coworkers began to ask questions. They eventually grew more suspicious when, despite the layers of makeup I applied, the bruises under my eyes showed through. Jay always avoided bruising my face or causing injuries that could be noticeable to others, but every once in a while he was careless. However, most of the time I suffered from fractures, large lumps on my skull, and bruises under my clothing that no one would ever see.

After a long day at work, I made the walk back home. It was only about one mile, but it aggravated me that I even had to walk at all. We had a car and a truck and both were registered under my name, but Jay made sure that neither of them would start for me. Or he'd keep the keys hidden.

This afternoon, when I arrived at our set of stairs, I looked up at my door, and something unusual caught my eye. I walked up to the second floor and stood at my doorstep. Jay had installed a camera system. I looked up at the big black camera staring down at me. I then took a deep breath and entered the apartment.

I stepped inside to see loose wires hanging from the wall. It was clear Jay installed the camera himself and didn't do a very good job at it.

"Hi," he said as he stepped into the living room. "You like the camera? Now I'll know exactly when you leave the house and exactly when you come back," he said with a grin.

I felt exhausted, so I kept quiet and walked into the bedroom. I wasn't concerned about the camera; in fact, I thought it was helpful. There was no way he could blame me for these outlandish accusations if he saw that I was home. Of course he would then accuse me of doing something else during work hours or on my walk back home. But at least the camera would take care of the rest of the day.

The more difficult things got at home, the more I began to read my Bible. I had a real desire to know God, but I think more than anything I was desperate for something to give me direction. Some days I'd read for hours, searching for answers. I felt more peace from God, but simultaneously, I felt stronger adversity coming from every other angle. Jay became even more hateful and angry toward me, and after months of struggling on my own, I felt completely helpless. I decided I needed to tell someone what was happening.

Chapter 39

I had now been attending church alone for a while, and each week Javier, the youth pastor, made it a point to come over and say hello and ask me how I was doing. I always kept my answers short, but there were times he would look me in the eyes and ask me a second time, like he knew I wasn't telling him something.

One morning after service, I waved at Javier from a distance. "Hi, can I talk with you for a few minutes?" I asked him.

"Of course! Let's sit down."

We walked to a quiet spot and took a seat. I began to tell him about Jay's anger and how he would often lose his temper when he was upset. I didn't tell him exactly how bad things were, and I was vague about what was actually taking place. I did, however, tell him about the drugs that I had found.

"Jessica, this is not good. We have to do something about this," he said. "I'm very concerned for you. Is there something I can do to help?"

"Pray for me, for us. I don't know what to do."

"What about if I come over? I can sit down with the two of you. We can talk, and I'll pray for you both."

I hesitated. I knew there was a chance Jay wouldn't like that, but I also knew that I had no one else to go to for help. I figured this was the kind of thing a church was for.

"Okay, let's do that."

I thanked him, and we agreed that he would come over the following evening.

The next morning, I told Jay that Javier offered to come over and pray for us. I was nervous because I knew he didn't particularly like Javier. I also didn't want him to feel attacked by us in any way so I made light of the situation.

"I guess he does this sort of thing all the time. I thought it could be a good idea!"

"I don't like Javier, and you know that. Are you stupid?"

I would've said anything at this point to make Jay agree to the visit.

"I'm sorry. I don't care much for him either, but I thought it was nice for him to offer."

Jay sighed. "Whatever. As long as it's quick, but you better not ever plan something like this again without asking me first."

The next day, right before Javier was supposed to arrive, Jay was irritable. I started to worry if I made a mistake, but I was so desperate for any help I could get. Even if the outcome wasn't what I hoped, I had to try. I heard a knock. I said a prayer in my head as I walked to the door.

"Hi!" I greeted Javier.

Jay stood in the living room with his arms crossed.

"Hi, brother," Javier said as he walked in.

Javier walked into the living room. Jay shook his hand but didn't say anything back to him. Then we all took a seat at the dining room table.

Javier began with a prayer and then asked Jay and me to each explain the challenges we were facing. I went first, but I was very careful about what I said.

"I feel that Jay and I need more of God in our lives. I also feel like our relationship needs help."

I was scared to say more than that. I didn't want to do anything that would provoke Jay or make him feel disrespected in front of Javier.

"Okay, Jessica. That's great to know." He turned to Jay. "Jay, what about you?"

"I don't have anything to say." He sat with his hands folded on the table.

"Are you sure there's nothing you'd like to talk about?" I asked him kindly.

"No!" he said.

I said nothing more. I knew he was on the verge of losing his temper. I looked over at Javier and prayed that he wouldn't say anything that would provoke him. The room felt tense.

"Brother, I want you to know that I'm here to help you just as much as much as I'm here to help Jessica. But I have to tell you, you need to treat your wife with respect."

I could feel my heart throbbing in my throat. I couldn't believe he said that to Jay.

"Who the hell do you think you are?"

"Brother, I have to be honest with you. I don't like the tone you have with Jessica." As much as I appreciated Javier speaking up for me, he needed to stop.

Jay stood up. "Get out of my house. Right now," he said. His voice was low and menacing.

"I don't mean to upset you, but you need to hear these things."

I prayed he would stop talking. Jay stepped closer to Javier.

"If you don't get out of my house right now, you'll need an ambulance to come get you out."

I knew Jay meant it. Javier quickly gathered his things from the table. I felt horrible; I knew this was my fault. Javier walked toward the door but stopped midway and turned around.

"Jay, I can see that you have anger. Be sure that you do not take it out on your wife."

Jay charged toward Javier.

"Stop!" I shouted.

Jay's fist was clenched, and he was about to beat Javier the same way he beat me.

"Javier, leave!" I yelled.

Javier opened the door and rushed out. Now it was just me with him.

"You're so stupid!" He screamed. I could feel his breath on my face. "I've never met anyone so stupid in my life!"

I kept quiet. I fully expected Jay to hit me, but he didn't. Instead, he walked into the bedroom. I felt like it was Javier's prayers that kept me safe that night.

The next day, when I got home from work, I wasn't as fortunate. I suppose Jay had time to ruminate on what had happened the night before and wanted to punish me for it. I could tell he was angry with me so I stayed away from him. After about an hour, when I thought he would leave me alone for the night, he came into the living room and stood in front of me as I sat on the couch.

"Do you have anything to say about yesterday?"

I thought carefully about what I should say next. I looked up at him, not yet sure what to say that would help me in this moment. Just then, he lunged toward me. With both of his hands, he grabbed me by my hair and shook me back and forth as if I were weightless. Then, he shoved me back into the couch, and with his right hand punched the front and sides of my head. One by one I felt the impact of his fist beating into my skull.

Both fists hit me on the left, then the right. Over and over. Then he threw me onto the floor. I don't have any recollection of the next several minutes, but I do recall suddenly feeling blows to my arms and back. Parts of my body began to feel numb as he continued to hit me. I lay on the floor, waiting for Jay to be finished.

Jay got off of me and left the room. Soon after, I felt Bruce licking my hand. I opened my eyes to see him standing over me. His ears were back as he looked down at me. I gently pulled him in closer to me and cried as I held him.

Minutes later, I watched Jay do the most horrifying thing I had ever seen him do. Jay walked back into the living room, reached down to grab Bruce, and then threw him against the wall. I wailed and screamed. I screamed as loud as I could, hoping someone would call the police.

Bruce whimpered as he hit the floor. Then he crawled over to me and hid himself in my arms as he shook uncontrollably. It killed me inside. I had to find a way for Bruce and me to leave.

Minutes later, there was a knock at our door.

"If you make a sound, I'll hurt you like you've never felt before," he whispered as he clenched his teeth. I held Bruce in my arms and didn't make a sound.

"This is the police department, open up."

Jay glared at me. I stayed silent. I wished that they would just bust through the door. We both sat still, looking at the door. Then, after a couple more knocks, they gave up and left.

Chapter 40

Jay told me that if I ever went to the police, it would be the biggest regret of my life. I believed him. I wondered how I could possibly get out of this relationship. The apartment, the two cars, and all the bills were in my name, and I had a job that I couldn't afford to leave. He knew where my friends lived as well as my mother. Jay knew everything I did and where I was at every minute of the day. I felt I had nowhere safe to go. I needed time to come up with a plan.

I felt that the situation I was in couldn't possibly get worse, but I found out that I was wrong. One evening, Jay came back up to the apartment after being downstairs in the garage for hours.

"I have something to show you," he said.

He walked past me and went into the bedroom. I stayed on the couch, thinking he was going to come back out. Then he peeked his head around the corner.

"Get in here," he said, smiling.

I was scared, and my body was trembling, but I got up.

"Sit right here, next to me." He playfully patted the bed and chuckled.

I sat on the edge of the bed and waited. Jay put in a DVD, then sat back down. I looked at the screen, waiting for whatever it was he was going to play. I could see him in the corner of my eye, watching me.

"You ready for this?" he asked.

I didn't respond to him, and suddenly, the DVD began playing.

"What is this?" I asked confused.

"Keep watching!" he said sternly.

Pornography played on the screen in front of me.

"I'm not watching this with you!" I stood up to leave the room, but before I could, Jay grabbed my wrist and yanked me back down.

"You have anything to say?"

"About what?" Tears filled my eyes. I was frustrated and exhausted.

"That's you." He smiled at me. I stared back at him blankly. "That's you," he said again. He stood up and pointed to the screen. "Right there, you slut!"

"Are you being serious? Do you think that's me?" I stared at him, dumbfounded.

"Yes, it's you. You dyed your hair for this video, but it's clearly you."

I stared back at him speechless. "Jay, you've lost your mind." I didn't shout, and I wasn't even angry in the moment. Instead, what I felt was extreme concern for his mental state. I was witnessing Jay hallucinating right in front of me.

"Jay, we need to get you help," I said as calmly as I could. Then I stood up to leave. I wasn't going to watch this any longer.

But as soon as I stood up, he grabbed me by my hair and threw me down onto the bed.

"You didn't think I'd ever find out, did you?" he said as he leaned down and squeezed my face, "Now keep watching it!" He gripped my shirt and sat me upright.

"Take your eyes off the screen one more time and I will beat you."

For the next couple of minutes, I watched what was playing in front of me while Jay taunted me and called me a whore. Finally, I looked away from the screen. I couldn't watch any more.

"Watch it!" he yelled. He gripped my hair and pointed my face toward the TV.

"Does it bother you seeing yourself on TV doing these things?"

"This isn't me," I cried.

"You're disgusting. How can a whore like you go to church and read your Bible?" He laughed. "You think you've got us all fooled, but I'm gonna tell everyone about this."

"This isn't me!" I shouted.

"Shut up and look at the TV!"

At that moment, I no longer cared what Jay did to me. I turned my face away from the TV and looked at him.

"I'm not scared of you, and I'm not watching this," I said to him.

He stood up, stepped in front of me, grabbed me from the bed, and then threw me down onto the floor. He then ripped off all my clothes until I was lying there naked.

With both fists, he punched my skull repeatedly. I could feel the impact of his fists hitting the sides of my face, and my ears burned from the repeated blows.

He then flipped me over onto my stomach and began punching me, making his way from my shoulder blades down to my lower back. A blow to my kidneys caused me to wail with pain. After my back, he worked his way back up to my head once more. He then ripped my body off of the floor and threw me back onto the bed. He positioned my body directly in front of the TV. He forced me to continue watching while he examined my body and compared what he was seeing on the screen to me. He insisted with certainty that my body, even down to the freckles on my skin, were the same as the woman in the video. Then, he pushed my upper body down so I lied flat. Then he raped me.

Minutes later, Jay threw me off the bed and onto the floor again. My head throbbed with excruciating pain, and I could feel the aching from the other parts of my body that had been hit. I lay there on the bedroom floor, unable to move, speak, or open my eyes. I couldn't imagine being in more pain than what I was in at that moment. I heard Jay's voice in the background, but I was too disoriented to know what he was saying. It took every bit of strength I had left, but I raised my voice to speak.

"I need a hospital," I said.

"Oh, shut up! You think you're hurting now. Just wait." He leaned in and punched the side of my skull again.

The pain was agonizing, and I'm uncertain how long I lay on the floor or if I went unconscious at any point, but eventually, after some time had passed, I attempted to get up. Carefully, I lifted my upper body and held myself up with both of my arms. Once the pounding in my head lessened, I slid myself over to the bed and rested my weight against the mattress. The movement caused the throbbing in my head to intensify, so I leaned my head back and closed my eyes. The pain was too piercing for me to lift myself up again and get into the bed. As I sat there, Jay came into the room and sat down at the edge of the bed.

"I should go to a hospital," I said under my breath.

"I'm not taking you to a hospital. You're not even that hurt!" he shouted.

I opened my eyes slightly to look at him as he spoke.

"If I really wanted to hurt you that bad, I would! You're fine!"

As Jay was shouting, I saw Bruce peek his head around the doorway. His ears were back, and he looked scared, but he began to crawl over to me. He cowered down as he hurried past Jay. His body was trembling uncontrollably. He then slowly crawled up onto my lap and spread all four of his legs out across me. I could feel him shaking. Bruce had heard the yelling so he came in to protect me from being hit. I looked down at what he had done, and I cried. I had never seen a more loving act in my life.

"He's trying to protect me from you," I said under my breath.

"Yeah, he is." Jay laughed. He got up and left the room while Bruce and I sat on the floor together.

With my body weak and tired, I finally got off of the floor and crawled into bed. As my heartbeat quickened, the pressure in my head intensified. I let out deep breaths to slow my heart rate. I practiced inhaling, then exhaling, until I drifted off to sleep.

The next morning, I woke early to the sound of my alarm. No matter what had happened the night before and no matter how much pain I was in, I had to go to work. I had rent that needed to be paid and groceries to buy.

With a migraine and a body riddled with aches and pain, it took me longer than usual to get out of bed. Nervous to see my own face in the mirror, I stepped into the bathroom, and I prepared to see the damage done. I looked up and saw my reflection. I then stepped closer to examine my face. Both of my eyes were swollen and bloodshot, and under my left eye were broken blood vessels showing through the skin.

Next, I looked down at my cheeks, which were covered in bloody scratches. With both hands, I then gently pulled my hair back, which revealed more injuries. Both of my ears were purple and swollen, and the same scratches that were on my face were on my neck. I stepped back and took a long look at my reflection. Tears filled my eyes as I looked at myself. I didn't know who I was anymore or how I got in this irreparable place.

I began to gently run my fingertips along my scalp to feel large knots all over my head, which felt like golf balls under my skin.

I applied layers of concealer to mask the discolorations on my face, but no matter how much I put on, some of the blood spots and scratches still peeked through. To hide my swollen ears, I put my hair in a low ponytail. Then I began to slowly get dressed, sitting down regularly to catch my breath.

Once dressed, I stood back and took another look at myself. I could see a long bright scratch peeking through from under my collar. I brought my ponytail over to the side to hide it, and then after one last look at myself, I headed out the door.

The next few days were a blur of serving tables, popping aspirin, and sleeping as soon as I got home. I tried to avoid any confrontation with Jay, which was easy because he was gone for two days. This time alone allowed me to recover and build my strength up.

Later that week, in the midst of all the stress of trying to work to pay the bills, I came home to an unexpected blessing at my door. As I walked up my stairs and approached my doorstep, I saw heaps of bags sitting on the ground. I looked closer and saw that the bags were filled with groceries. There must have been six or seven bags. Attached was a little note: "Blessings to you, Jessica." There was no name written at the bottom.

I was overwhelmed with gratitude. It couldn't have come at a better time. Money was always tight so the fridge was always bare. I bought as much food as I could with the money I had, but with Jay always taking my tips out of my purse, I never had enough money to keep much food in the house.

I'd find out the next day at work that the groceries were dropped off by my coworker, Lauren. She and I had been slowly getting to know each other over the past couple of months, and despite me not opening up to her about my situation, she said she knew I could use the help.

It was 3:00 a.m. when suddenly I was woken by our bedroom light being turned on.

"Time for you to wake up," Jay uttered under his breath.

I began to open my eyes just slightly to see him standing above the bed. Then, before I knew what was going on, he ripped the blanket off of me.

"Please stop. Let me sleep," I cried out.

He bent down and gripped my shirt with both of his hands. He pulled me close to him so that we were face-to-face. His eyes were wide, and I could tell that he'd been using drugs all night. I felt weak. I didn't feel like fighting back. I prayed that he would stop so I could go back to sleep.

"Every morning and every night, I'm gonna make your life hell for all the times you've lied to me."

I felt hopeless and defeated. I said nothing. I had no fight in me.

He lifted my body from the bed and threw me down. Pain shot through my body as all of my weight hit the floor. My head pounded violently.

He hit the side of my face and back of my head. Whatever may have happened after this, I don't recall.

It had been weeks since I had had a real conversation with my mother. Each time we spoke, I would tell her that I was either about to start my shift or that I was busy. I couldn't tell her the truth; I was so ashamed and scared. But, inevitably she became suspicious. I could tell by her recent voicemails.

"Jess, I'm gettin' worried about you. I never hear from you anymore. Let me know that everything is okay with you."

I knew I had to call her, but Mom could always read people well, and she saw through lies easily. So, the next day, I put on a performance of phony laughter and a fake story of how I've been too busy to call. Mom seemed happy yet surprised to hear from me. She asked all the questions I had expected: "Why haven't I been hearing from you?", "How are you and Jay?", and "Are you sure everything's okay?" I said everything I needed to put her mind at ease.

We talked for several more minutes, and by the end of the conversation, I felt exhausted from the energy it took to make the call. But I knew my mother needed to hear from me, and it wasn't right for me to ignore her.

When we hung up, I was pretty certain that she had no idea what was really going on in my life.

I prayed every day. It was the one thing I clung to that helped me get through my days, and it was one of the only things that gave me any encouragement. I wasn't going to church as much because I didn't have a way to get there. Jay was still hiding the keys from me, or he'd remove a part from under the hood so the car wouldn't start. Every once in a while, however, he would forget to do these things, and I'd be able to go.

I looked back on all of this, and I wondered how many times God had given me an opportunity to leave Jay, and I didn't. I wondered how much of this was my own fault. I had so many fears. No matter how hard I tried, I couldn't see a safe way out. Everything I had worked hard for I would lose, and no matter where I escaped to, I knew that Jay would find me.

Days later I came home from work to see my Bible lying open on the countertop. I loved this Bible. I spent hours each week reading it, and Jay knew it was the one thing I had that I cherished. With a yellow highlighter and ballpoint pen, he wrote all over the pages. Verses were underlined, and any blank space on the pages were now filled with the words "whore" and "liar." Where there were verses speaking about wives, he highlighted them and left his own commentary on the edges. He wrote things like, "This is how a wife is supposed to act," and "Pray for forgiveness about all the rotten things you've done." His writing was slashed all across the pages. I was angry, and it made me want to throw my Bible in the garbage. But I knew that Jay wanted to ruin every enjoyable thing I had in my life, and I wouldn't let him take this. So I kept it, and every day when I opened my Bible and read, instead of looking at his writing and highlighted verses with resentment, I looked at them knowing that those verses *did* describe who I was and that I was loved by God.

My life was in a downward spiral, leading me to destruction and perhaps even death, but somehow I still had hope.

Chapter 41

Late one night, about one week later, Jay was sleeping in bed next to me. I dozed off, then shortly after was woken up by the sound of him gasping for air. It sounded like he was suffocating. I sat up and looked at him. The room was dark, but I could see that he had his own two hands wrapped around his throat.

"Help me!" he gasped.

"Jay?" I said as I shook him. I didn't know what was happening. I assumed he was having a nightmare.

"Help me," he said louder.

"Jay!"

Finally, he took in a big breath of air, and removed his hands from his throat and looked over at me.

"You couldn't help me?" he shouted.

"How was I supposed to help you? You had your hands around your throat."

"I was being choked. I was trying to take its hands off of me, you're so stupid!"

"What? Who was choking you?"

"I don't know! But you didn't do a damn thing!"

He sighed loudly, ripped the covers off me, rolled over, and went back to sleep.

After the days of being beaten, there were days of silence. Days when Jay disappeared or simply stayed in the garage all day and night. Every so often he'd get arrested for possession, and I knew I'd have a couple days of peace. I cherished the times when I could be alone. On the days when Jay didn't hit me, he'd instead make me endure agonizing conversations with him. He'd put me through hours of questioning and arguing.

One night, after Jay had been taunting me, I was so fed up with him that I told him I was going to walk to the payphone at the gas station and call my mother. Jay had taken my phone away from me at this point, so for the past couple of weeks I had to walk to the Chevron if I wanted to make any calls.

"Oh, it's okay. I'll drive you," he said sarcastically.

But I wanted to get away from him. "No, I'll walk. I don't want to be around you."

"Oh, so you can go call one of your boyfriends?" He laughed. "Yeah, right, like I'll sit at home for that. I'll take you."

I wanted to speak to Mom alone. I wanted to open up to her about some things that were going on, but now I wouldn't be able to speak as honestly to her.

Before Jay would drive me to the gas station, he decided he wanted to take a shower. This was just another way for him to irritate me, but I was too scared to go against what he said and go to the phone without him so I waited. But then once his shower was finally over, he stayed in the bathroom for over an hour. His plan worked; I got angry.

"Get out of the bathroom and take me to the phone."

He didn't respond. I pounded on the door. I heard him utter something under his breath.

"Get out of the bathroom!" I said to him. But he didn't respond. I stood there, fuming with anger until, finally, I kicked the bathroom door in.

"What the hell are you doing, Jessica?" I didn't respond to him. Instead, I kicked the door in again and again. Until, at last, it was hanging from its hinges. He stood wrapped in his towel. He looked at me and then at the door.

"Take me to the phone," I said once more.

I stood back and looked at the ruined door. I felt satisfied with myself. I took a seat at the table while he got dressed.

Jay didn't have anything to say to me so we walked down to the truck in silence. About three minutes later, we were at the gas station.

"Finally," I said under my breath as we pulled up to the payphone. He parked the truck, and I hopped out, and so did he.

"I'm coming to listen to your call to make sure you're actually talking to your mom," he said.

Together, we walked up to the phone, and I began to dial her number.

"You're not even dialing your mom's number, you liar!"

"What are you talking about? Get back in the truck."

"No," he said. I looked back at the phone and continued to dial.

"Who are you really calling?" he asked me.

I slammed the phone down. "Watch carefully, Jay, because I'm only gonna do this once."

Again, and slowly, I began to dial. "209," I said loudly and sarcastically while I pressed the digits.

He watched me carefully as I dialed. The phone began to ring, and I wished more than anything that she would pick up. Jay leaned in close so he could hear.

"Hello?"

"Hi, Mom. It's Jess."

"Hey, Jess. Is everything okay?"

I turned my body away so Jay couldn't listen in on my mom.

"Yeah, I'm calling you from a payphone because Jay won't let me use my own phone." He let out a small laugh. "I'd like to come stay with you for a couple of days."

"Okay. Is he with you right now?" she asked quietly.

"Yes."

She played it cool, knowing there was a chance he could hear her. "Okay, Jess, well, I'm sure that you two will work it out, but I'd love for you to come visit."

"Okay, that would be nice. I'm gonna have Jay give me one of the cars so I can come out there."

My mother had no idea that Jay kept both vehicles from me. This was my way of telling her.

"Okay, Mom. I'll call you tomorrow and let you know when I'm coming out there."

"Okay, Jess, I love you. Be careful."

Even in my frustration, I realized I couldn't tell my mother about the abuse until I knew I was ready to leave it all behind for good. If she and my brother found out, they'd never allow me to go back home, and I didn't want to leave my home, my job, and my life. For this reason, I decided to not visit Mom and talk to her like I had planned.

Chapter 42

Each day was harder than the last, and I wondered how much longer I could continue living this way. Or living at all. My body couldn't take many more nights of senseless beatings, and my mind couldn't take the torment. I never knew leaving would be so hard. I didn't love him anymore, but fear kept me there. The stories of his past played in my mind. The stories he told me about the ways he had gotten back at people who had wronged him. I knew he was capable of anything. I was sure he would come after me once I left, and he would find me.

What was I supposed to do? Was God telling me something, but I wasn't hearing Him? Had He made a way out that I had overlooked? I was desperate for answers, and I felt in my heart that I would die in my apartment if I didn't find a way out.

After weeks of more paranoia and delusions, I urged Jay once again to see someone for help. He refused and insisted that the only one who needed help was me. But I grew concerned for the people around Jay; he was a danger to everyone he encountered. His temper overflowed onto random strangers in the store and other drivers on the road. One week before, as we were leaving the bank, he backed out of his parking spot, neglecting to check his mirrors, and he hit a car that was passing behind us.

It was Jay's fault, and he knew it, but instead of him apologizing to the man, he went up to the car and began screaming at him. The man, who had already stepped out of his car, rushed to get back inside. When he did, Jay screamed at him louder. Then he punched the man's door and hood, leaving crater-like dents all over the car.

I watched all of this through the window of the truck. I felt horrible for the man. I could see him holding his phone, frantically calling the police.

Jay walked back over to the truck. "Take the blame for the accident," he told me.

"No, I don't even have insurance." Our car insurance had recently lapsed due to me not being able to make my payment.

He looked me in the eyes. "Get in the driver's seat."

I did what he said. I moved over to the driver's seat and waited for the police to arrive.

At the end of it, my license was revoked for one year, and I was given a bill of approximately $2,765 for the damage to the man's car.

After another long day on my feet, I started my walk home. I walked slowly. The sky was beautiful that evening, like a blue canvas striped with layers of pink, purple, and orange. It seemed strangely quiet and peaceful. Somehow the loud, busy streets looked different after walking them lonely and tired. I appreciated peaceful moments like these.

As I stepped into the apartment complex, I could no longer see the painted sky. The brief feeling of peace I had was now gone, and my anxiousness rushed back.

I walked past the five or six buildings on the way to mine. I reached building twelve and paused at the bottom of the stairs. I hoped Jay wouldn't be home when I opened the door.

I unlocked the door and walked inside. Bruce scampered over to me with his tail wagging. I scooped him up in my arms and rocked him back and forth as his face was up against mine. With my apron and work clothes still on, we sat on the floor together, and after fifteen minutes, Bruce hadn't left my lap. Just then, Jay walked out of the bedroom and sat on the couch. I knew he was there to question me about my day, and I was tired.

"Leave me alone. I'm not in the mood to talk to you about anything," I said to him.

I knew I shouldn't talk to Jay in that tone, but I was tired and I didn't care. He got up and walked toward me, causing Bruce to immediately leap off my lap and hide near the couch.

Jay gripped a handful of my hair, then hit me in the face, dislocating my jaw. Then he picked me up and threw my body onto the ground.

Suddenly, Jay stood up and headed for the bathroom. When he walked back out, he had something hidden behind him. He walked up to me, then gripped all of my hair from behind me. Then I felt cold metal on the back of my neck.

"What're you doing?" I screamed.

I reached back to grab my hair out of his hands, then I felt a pair of scissors. Just then, I began to hear the sound of my hair being sliced between the blades, and my hair began to fall. It trickled down my arms and lay at my feet.

I struggled to get away from him, but he clenched my hair tightly in his hands. The scissors weren't sharp enough to cut through the thick chunk of hair, so he threw them to the ground and dragged me into the kitchen. He ripped open a drawer and pulled out a steak knife. He began to slice through my hair as if he were cutting through a piece of meat. He held my head firm with his left hand, and I cried as I felt the blade graze the back of my neck. Then he worked his way up toward my ears. I begged him to stop. I could feel the cold metal against my ears, and I felt more of my hair fall onto my shoulders. He took one last hack through the hair I had left, then he tossed the knife onto the kitchen table.

I reached back with both hands to feel the bare skin of my neck. My fingertips slowly took in the new rigid edges of my chopped hair. I fell to the floor and cried as I looked at my long, beautiful hair that was scattered across the carpet.

"Get in the shower!" he demanded.

I didn't move or respond. I held my hair in my hands and cried.

"Get your ass in the shower!" he shouted again.

I turned around and looked at him. "Why do you need me to take a shower?" I asked nervously.

He turned to me and paused. Jay hated being questioned. "I'm not gonna tell you again."

Before I had the chance to stand up, Jay walked toward me and ripped me up off the floor. His nails dug into my skin as he squeezed my arm. He dragged me into the bathroom and stripped my clothes off of me. Then he lifted me up and threw me into the shower. My back slammed against the wall, and my body writhed as it hit the floor. The impact from the fall sent severe pain down my leg.

He reached over and turned the knob; water began to pour over me as I lay there. He then slammed the bathroom door shut as he walked out. I felt the water turn scalding hot so I reached over quickly and adjusted the temperature.

I sat beneath the water and wept from the deepest parts of me. I wanted to leave, and I hated myself for being a coward. It wasn't who I was raised to be. I never thought I'd be one of those girls I heard about that gets trapped in an abusive relationship. Not me. I was too smart for that. But here I was.

I wasn't sure what was worse: the mental abuse or being hit. Not being able to chew my food because of a dislocated jaw or the panic attacks and unceasing nightmares. Physical pain is tangible, but mental and emotional pain creeps up on you in ways you never expect. And somehow it's the emotional pain that shows itself to others far more than the bruises do, and the emotional scars go far deeper than the physical ones. Somehow, my life had become one of merely surviving, one of abuse and chaos, just like the life I vowed to escape from when Paul and I were kids.

Minutes later, I heard my name being called. I shut off the water and stepped out of the shower. I was terrified of what was waiting for me on the other side of the door.

I tiptoed out of the bathroom with a towel wrapped around me. I peeked into the bedroom as I came out; I didn't see Jay. I walked into the living room and peeked around the corner.

Then Jay came up behind me and shoved me onto the floor. I crawled away from him while holding my towel around me. He walked over to me, got down on his knees, and came in close.

"Please don't hurt me," I pleaded.

He stared at me and paused. There was only silence between us. His lips were tightly shut, and the breathing through his nose was becoming heavier and louder. He opened his mouth to speak as his teeth were clenched together. Only his lips moved. Then in a low calm voice, he said something that he had never said to me before. "You're going to die tonight."

I looked back at him; tears cascading down my face. He leaned in closer, gazing at me. Suddenly, I witnessed something I had never seen before, something that words will never be able to describe. It was as if I were looking into the eyes of a demon.

I wasn't dealing with Jay in this moment; it was something much scarier. He stared into my eyes but said nothing. It felt like time had stopped. Terror overwhelmed me; I began to crawl backward to get away from him. But I could only go so far as my back hit the coffee table behind me.

"Please don't hurt me!" I cried out.

I knew this was it. I was about to endure something more horrific than I ever had. Jay grabbed me by my ankles and dragged me across the floor. My towel slid off of me as he moved me into the hallway. He flipped me onto my stomach, then held me down and sat on my lower back. With my arm behind my back, he gripped my elbow, shoving my arm upward, as high as it would go, threatening to break it. The pain was unbearable.

"Admit that that was you in the video, or I'll break your arm," he said as he slowly applied more and more pressure.

I felt something in my arm slowly tear, and I begged him to stop. I squirmed to try to gain relief. He flipped me onto my back, then sat his 211-pound body on my chest. He placed one of his knees on my right wrist and the other knee on my left wrist. I was pinned down, unable to use my hands or move my body. I was completely defenseless.

He raised his fist into the air, and I closed my eyes. Left, then right, his fists struck my face and skull. I believe I lost consciousness briefly.

Just inches away from me, there was a small cabinet. It was wooden and had sharp pointed corners at the bottom that protruded from all four sides.

With one hand, Jay dug his fingers into my cheeks, then turned my face to the left, facing the cabinet. He pushed my body closer, then placed the temple of my head against the pointed corner of the cabinet. Then, he placed both of his hands on the right side of my head, and using his weight, he pressed down on my face. The wooden corner pressed hard into my head. Gradually, I felt more and more pressure. I began to wail and squirm, but he used his right hand to cover my mouth. I could feel the sharp point digging into my head, and the pressure became more than I could bear.

With one last push, he pressed his weight onto my head, then released. My eyes rolled to the back of my head, and I closed my eyes. The next several minutes were a blur. I don't remember what took place immediately after this.

Soon, however, I could hear Jay's voice as he still sat on my chest. It seemed he was shaking me to get my attention. Next, he took both of his palms and placed one on each side of my head. Then, with all his might, he pushed in on my head from both sides as if his hands were a vice. As if he were attempting to crush in my skull.

"Stop," I whispered.

It felt as if at any moment my skull would shatter under the pressure. It took effort for me to lift open my eyelids enough to look at him. But when I did, he looked right at me. His face was scrunched in anger, and I could see the vein in his forehead as he strained. I felt my eyes roll back and whatever took place next is a blur.

The next thing I remember is Jay letting out a loud sigh as he finally released his grip. I didn't have the strength to move or speak. I wondered what damage had been done and if I were dying.

My head lay on the carpet, and I used all the energy I had to try to open my eyes, but the pain was excruciating. Every inch of my body was in agony. Beyond the pain in my head, I could hear his voice as I felt his weight on my chest. I opened my eyes, but only for a moment, until they rolled back again. I felt him lean in close to me and his breath on my face. He sat very still. I wondered if he were checking my breathing. Then, seconds later, his fists started pounding my head, my chest, and my arms.

I felt myself slipping in and out of consciousness. I yearned to sleep. I wondered if I surrendered to the urge, would I ever wake up again? Visions of my mother and Paul played in my mind. For them, I couldn't let myself go. As well as I could, I focused my thoughts on speaking to God.

God, make him stop.

I could feel the blows, but all was silent around me.

God, please make him stop.

"I hate you!" I could hear Jay screaming at me as I lay there.

Suddenly, I felt no more pain. It was as if my body had shut down. I was ready to surrender.

Jesus, let it be finished. Take care of my mom and Paul. Make sure they know that I loved them.

My mind felt like it was shutting down. All of my senses had shut off, and I felt like I was all alone in a dark, quiet room. I was twenty-one years old, and this was it; I was ready to go. I felt out of my body as I could no longer feel anything.

Then, for a moment, the feeling in my body and the clarity in my mind came back to me. I opened my eyes just slightly. I saw Jay's fists hitting my body, although I didn't feel it. My head rolled back, and my eyes closed. I waited for that last blow that would end my life.

Then, with strength in me that I didn't know I had, I said a simple prayer to God. I didn't speak out loud; I simply thought it. It wasn't a request; instead, it was my final words to God.

Days before this, I had written down a Bible verse that read, "Never will I leave you; never will I forsake you." This verse came to mind as I lay there on the floor. I spoke to God one last time.

But God, you said, "Never will I leave you; never will I forsake you."

What happened next was beyond anything I could ever explain. Suddenly, the hitting stopped and Jay threw his fists into the air. It was as if his hands were torn off of me. I began to open my eyes and look up at him. He was staring down at me. His eyes were wide as if he had seen a ghost. He didn't speak a word to me. Instead, he sat there while both of his palms were raised up high in the air. He stared at me and was silent. Then, he got off of me and got into bed.

Chapter 43

I couldn't explain what happened, but I knew God saved me. It looked and felt as if someone had torn Jay's hands off of me. I didn't move; I didn't have the strength. I continued to lay on the floor. My head throbbed violently, and there was a sharp pain down my neck. My arms felt heavy and weak, and my back ached with large knots and bruises.

I lay there for several minutes. Then I heard Jay's voice as he called my name.

"Get in bed," he shouted.

With my body bloody and beaten, I could hardly move. But he called my name again, and I knew that I had to get up. I slowly rolled over and got on my hands and knees.

I was frightened to see myself in the mirror. I wondered if I would even recognize myself.

"Get in bed now!" he yelled again.

I lifted myself up and stood to my feet. Slowly and nervously, I walked into the bedroom. I kept my head down. I stretched one arm over my breasts and the other over my waist to cover my body as I staggered past him.

He was laying on the bed; his eyes were closed, and his arms were crossed over his chest. I kept my eyes on him as I made my way to my side of the bed. I pulled back the sheet and slowly crawled in. My left leg rested upon the edge of the mattress, nearly hanging from the bed. I wanted to be as far away from him as I possibly could.

Minutes later, Jay's eyes were still closed, and he hadn't made a single movement. He was pretending to be asleep. There was nothing more I wanted in that moment than to close my eyes. But I was too scared to go to sleep. I forced myself to stay awake and to think of ways that I could get out of the apartment. If I messed this up, I would pay for it. I had to be sure that I could make it out.

The front door was wedged closed, and there was no way for me to open it. A tabletop, made of a heavy slab of granite, was propped underneath the door handle. The position of it kept me from being able to move the door handle, and the weight of it prevented me from being able to lift it.

I thought about the sliding glass door in the living room and how he had broken the handle on it so I wasn't able to unlock and open it. The only other way out would be through the bedroom window. The hardest part would be sliding it open quickly enough for him to not hear or see me. Next, I'd have to take off the screen and then jump from the second floor. Whatever I decided to do, I had to go through with it because there would be no second chance for me to leave if Jay caught me.

Several more minutes had gone by, and he hadn't moved or made a sound. If I planned to make it out of here, I needed clothes.

"Jay?" I whispered.

"Why are you waking me up," he snapped back at me. His eyes remained closed as he lay there.

"My head is pounding. Can I get up for a glass of water?"

"Hurry up!" he said angrily.

I thought it was best that I earn his trust by grabbing water first. Plus, I needed to know if he were going to watch me walk to the kitchen. I needed to know what to expect from him when I got up the second time to leave.

I grabbed water from the kitchen and came straight back to bed. A wave of relief washed over me once I realized he hadn't moved from the bed, and he trusted me to do what I said I was going to do.

I set my glass down on my nightstand and lifted the sheets to get back in bed.

"Jay?"

"What now?"

"Can I put clothes on now? It's getting cold."

"No!"

"Okay, can I at least grab underwear?"

There was a long silence from him, then he let out a loud sigh.

"Fine, but hurry up!"

"Okay."

I got out of bed slowly, without any urgency. I didn't want to give him any reason to be suspicious of me. I walked over to the suitcase that sat on the floor near the front door. Jay had gathered my clothes and put them in a suitcase so I didn't have any of my clothes in the bedroom. Without clothes, he knew I couldn't leave. And if I were to try to get clothes, he would know I was planning to leave.

I glanced over toward the bedroom, then back down at the suitcase. I rummaged through the small amount of clothes that I had left and saw a pair of my jeans. If I put these on, I had to be fast, and I had to be ready to leave. I had to time this perfectly.

My heart was racing as I contemplated my next move. I knew that once he saw me with more than underwear on, he would know I was up to something. I had my hand on the jeans as I struggled to decide what to do.

Suddenly, as I was bent down with my hands in the suitcase, Jay took a step out of the bedroom. He stopped in his tracks, looked at me, and then flashed me a smile as he took a step forward into the bathroom. This was it. If I didn't get out of this apartment now, I never would.

I jumped to my feet as quickly as possible. I heard Jay loudly fumbling under the bathroom sink, and I knew he was in search of something to use on me, just like earlier with the scissors. Hastily, I pulled up my jeans. Just then, I heard the bathroom cabinet slam shut.

Without anything else on besides unzipped jeans, I reached for the slab of marble. I grabbed it with both hands, and I ripped it out from under the door handle. I threw it onto the floor, unlocked the deadbolt, and raced out of the front door. Without a bra or shirt, with pants unzipped, and barefoot, I ran down the two flights of stairs. Adrenaline pumped violently through my veins as I ran to save my own life. I ran fast without stopping and without looking behind me. I ran through building after building and through the well-lit areas, hoping someone would see me and help me. I didn't stop, fearing he was right behind me. Before I reached the end of the complex, I raced up a flight of stairs and pounded on the door of someone in building six. I knocked, frantically praying that the person on the other side would open up. I knew Jay would get to me at any second.

I heard noise from inside the apartment, but no one opened the door.

"Please open the door, I need help!" I pleaded with the stranger inside.

"Go away!"

"Please, I need help!" I pled softly.

"Go away!" they yelled back.

I ran down the stairs back to the first floor, and I knocked furiously on the next door that I saw.

"Get away from here!" the person yelled.

I looked all around me, then ran to the next door.

"Please open up. I need help!"

I heard noise from inside, but no one opened up.

Desperate, I ran to a different building. I realized that no one would answer the door to me if I knocked loudly. They were scared and thought I could be a threat.

I was now in the last building in the complex. I ran up the stairs and approached a door on the second floor. I took a deep breath and placed a very light knock at the door. A woman opened the door and stood before me wide-eyed.

"Oh my God!" she shrieked.

I stood before her with my chopped hair still wet from the shower. My upper body was naked, and I was without shoes or socks. My face was beaten, and my nose was lined with dried blood. My eyes were purple; deep scratches covered my face, neck, and arms, and my back was tender from bruises and lumps.

"Please let me use your phone, that's all I'm asking."

"Yes! Of course." The woman rushed back inside to get her phone.

Just then, another woman from inside came from around the corner. Her eyes widened as she placed her hand over her gaping mouth.

"Oh my God," she uttered.

The first woman quickly came back and gave me her phone.

"Thank you so much," I said to her.

I was so grateful they opened the door to me. The first woman stood with me as the second woman walked away and headed down the hall. I called my mother.

"Mom, I have never asked you for help, but I need you to drive to Antioch right now and get me."

It was now 9:00 p.m., and it was nearly an hour and a half drive for her. I knew she had a million questions, but she refrained from asking them and quickly agreed to come get me. As I hung up the phone, the second woman came back with socks in one hand and a T-shirt in the other.

"Please take these!"

I thanked her. Their kindness meant more to me than I could express in that moment. I handed the phone back to the woman while I put on the T-shirt and socks.

"Please tell me what happened to you," the first woman said.

I felt I owed her an answer, although I didn't want to talk about it.

"The guy I'm with did this to me." That was all I could muster up in that moment.

She stared back at me, not knowing what to say. I could see the horror on her face. The second woman stepped away again, then about a minute later came back.

"I notified the police. They'll be here any minute."

I panicked. The reality of what I was doing came crashing down on me. If I told the police that Jay was responsible for this, he'd find me, and he'd punish me. He promised me that.

The police would be arriving at any moment and what would I tell them? I was terrified of telling the truth. I knew Jay would retaliate against me for having him arrested, and the police wouldn't be able to protect me from him. Just then, the two patrol cars pulled up. I and the two women walked downstairs.

The women began explaining how I showed up at their door. One officer stepped aside with them, and another officer took me aside. My heart raced, and fear was the only thing I could feel in this moment.

"Ma'am, we should call you an ambulance."

My world was crashing down on me, and I was fighting to stay afloat. I didn't have health insurance, and I knew if they called an ambulance and took me to the hospital, I wouldn't have the money for the medical bills.

"No, officer. I don't have insurance to pay for all that. Do not call me an ambulance." He paused and looked at me with his arms folded.

"Tell me who did this to you."

I stood before the officer trembling, thinking of what Jay would do to me if I told the truth.

"Who's the guy responsible for this?"

I gave a phony name, and the officer stepped away for a minute, then came back.

"Where does he live?"

"Well, we just met. I'm not sure where he lives," I answered.

"What's his phone number?"

"I don't have my phone with me, and I don't have it memorized."

"So you don't know where he lives or how to reach him?"

"No, I'm sorry."

The officer sighed. "Okay, where do *you* live?"

"I live in these apartments actually."

"Which one?"

"1223."

The officer walked away and spoke to the others. I sat in the backseat of the patrol car while waiting for him to come back. Finally, after a little while, he walked back over to me.

"Okay, so we had one of our officers go to your apartment to check things out. We knew you weren't being truthful about what happened. We found Jay in the apartment, and he's gonna be taken into custody right now."

"If he thinks I turned him in, he's gonna come after me!"

"No, he knows you gave us a fake name." A wave of relief washed over me. "Now, your neighbor Kathy was outside as all this was goin on. She offered to take your dog until you come back home."

"Okay." I knew this was the best place Bruce could possibly be right now.

"Alright, well, let's get in the car, and I'll drive you to Chevron."

I waited in the backseat of the patrol car while the officer spoke to the cashier at Chevron. I didn't know what was said, but the young guy behind the counter unlocked the door for me to come in, and he had a chair set out for me to sit in.

"You keep yourself safe," the officer said to me.

He gave me a quick glance and then headed for the door. I'd now spend the next hour and thirty minutes in the bright fluorescent Chevron store.

The young cashier didn't speak a word to me, but every so often, I caught him looking over at me.

My chair was set in a place that wouldn't be easily seen from the night window when people walked up to pay. But as I watched him interact with customers, I could see some of them notice me. Their eyes would glance around the store as they waited for their change, and then they would spot me. Immediately, they'd look down once we made eye contact, but then, curious, they would always look at me again.

As I waited for my mother, the weight of the shame and embarrassment became harder to bear. Here I was sitting inside a gas station that I was escorted to by the police. My once long beautiful hair was chopped up to my ears, and I had no way to hide that from my mother when she arrived. I couldn't hide anything anymore.

Finally, I saw the headlights of her Ford Explorer pull up. I got up and walked toward the door, full of relief and dread all at the same time. I opened the door and looked back at the guy behind the counter.

"Thank you," I said. He didn't look me in the eyes or respond.

The headlights beamed on my face as I walked out. My brother was in the passenger seat. I knew their eyes were examining me. I kept my head down and got in the backseat. I breathed a sigh of relief once I was inside. I knew I was safe for now.

"Jess, you need to go to the hospital."

"No, Mom. I promise I'm fine. I just want to go to bed."

For the first couple of minutes, the ride was quiet. Then, my mother began her questions very gently. I told her I was tired, and she didn't pry. She knew that if she scared me off I would never ask for her help again. I was sure that she and Paul had spent the entire car ride to Antioch planning the best way to handle this. I lay down on the backseat and rested the whole way back to Turlock.

As soon as we got home, I lay down the couch. Mom brought me a blanket, and Paul gave me one of his pillows. I knew in the morning I would be confronted with their questions, but for now I'd rest.

The next morning, I woke up to the heavy realization of where I was and what happened the night before. Before I even opened my eyes, I was overwhelmed with dread and shame. I heard my mother in the kitchen cooking breakfast. She had decided to stay home from work that day. I kept my eyes closed and spent the next several minutes mentally preparing myself for what this day would bring.

I got up and wrapped myself with my blanket, trying to hide my short hair and bruises. I then went into Paul's room.

"Do you have a hoodie?" I asked him.

He looked at me and paused for a moment. It was the first time he was getting a good look at my face in the daylight. I knew he sensed that I wanted a hoodie to hide myself.

"Yeah, no problem."

He handed me a sweater and pretended to not even notice my face or my hair. In that moment, that was one of the kindest things he could've done for me.

I pulled the hoodie over me and then walked into the kitchen. Mom said good morning as she turned toward me. She stopped in her tracks for a moment when she saw my face. I looked back down and walked toward the kitchen table.

"I made eggs with biscuits and gravy." Her tone was upbeat, like she was trying. "Here let me get you some orange juice," she said cheerfully.

"Thanks, Mom."

She plated breakfast for the three of us, and we sat silently while we ate. None of us knew what to say or where to begin. Moments later, Paul attempted to lighten the mood with a joke; I couldn't help but smile.

Maybe everything is going to be okay after all, I thought.

Chapter 44

Mom finally began asking the questions I knew she was dying to ask. I didn't want to talk about any of it. I wasn't emotionally ready to reveal the truth. I didn't want to tell my mom about the horrific attack I experienced, or about how I lay on the floor unconscious and how these kinds of things had been taking place for a while but I was too scared to leave.

"Yes, Mom. Jay did this, but I'm not ready to talk about it." This was all I would give her, or anyone, at that moment.

Despite most of the injuries being hidden: traumatic brain injury, neck and rotator cuff injuries, and a body riddled with swelling and bruises, based off what she *could* see, Mom asked again to take me to the hospital. Regrettably, I refused.

Two days later, Mom's house phone rang. Mom stepped outside to answer, then several minutes later, she came in and handed me the phone. It was Jay. I didn't know that Jay had my mother's phone number, let alone had it memorized. I didn't know what my mother had said to him, but I could imagine.

I took the phone and walked outside.

"Hello? Baby?" he said.

I couldn't believe he had the nerve to call me that. I didn't respond.

"I'm not mad at you. I deserve this. I'm so sorry for what I've done to you."

I was quiet, and to be honest, I wasn't sure why I even took the call.

"I've been battling for a long time. I don't know what happened last night. I am so, so sorry. Me being in jail is the best thing possible. It'll give me time to think and pray again."

I was silent.

"Please say something," he said.

"I didn't give the police your name. I just want you to know that."

"It doesn't matter either way. This was a good thing."

"When you get out, you'll need another place to stay," I told him.

"Baby, I will never, ever, hurt you again, but I understand."

There was a long pause on both ends of the phone.

"I could be here a while, so if they ask you about pressing charges against me, make sure to tell them no, okay?"

I thought about if for a moment, pressing charges was exactly what I should've done, but the truth was that I was still scared of Jay.

"Okay," I said. *Maybe this way,* I thought, *we really can separate peacefully.*

Being at Mom's felt like a refuge, at first. There were home-cooked meals, restful sleep (despite nightmares reliving what had taken place days before), and peace and quiet. But within a few days, I was ready to go back home to Bruce. I had never relied on my mother for anything, but now I relied on her for everything. I didn't have a car so she had to take me places. I didn't have money, so she had to buy me the things I needed during my stay, and I didn't have my own phone. Thinking about it, I suppose this wasn't actually too different from my normal home life with Jay. Still, I didn't like relying on anyone else but myself, and I needed to go. I missed Bruce terribly, and I needed to go back to work before I lost my job.

Mom and Paul didn't like the idea of me going back, and they pleaded with me to stay longer. They even offered to help pay my bills for me. Even though I had kept the worst details to myself, I knew my mother sensed there was much more going on. But she knew I wasn't ready to tell her everything yet, and she knew that if she pushed too hard, I'd never ask her for help again. She walked on eggshells during all of this while I tried to figure it all out. I'm sure this was all very hard for her.

Despite being worried, Mom agreed that she'd take me back the following day as long as Jay wasn't going to be coming back to the apartment. I assured her that he wouldn't be.

The next day, I stepped inside my apartment and looked around at the damage that was left behind. After leaving, then coming back again, it looked and felt far more depressing than I remembered. I looked up at the damaged walls, the pile of my hair still on the carpet, and my towel still lying in the same place on the floor as when it was pulled off me.

I thought to myself how this was my second chance. I had found a way to keep my apartment and my independence while also getting rid of Jay.

I opened up the blinds and started to clean up. Shortly after, I went to Kathy's to get Bruce. We talked; she prayed for me, and she begged me to be careful.

"When he gets out, he's gonna get his clothes and stay somewhere else," I assured her.

"You think he'll really stay away from you?" she asked, doubtful.

"Yes, I really do. Plus, he's not gonna want to go back to jail, and now he knows that my family knows what he's done."

I felt like Jay knew better than to ever touch me again. After being arrested and my family finding out, I believed he'd leave me alone.

Despite missing a week of shifts, the restaurant let me keep my job. And as much as I tried to keep my personal life private, I owed an apology to my manager. He was kind and said that the team missed me. He agreed to put me back on the schedule right away.

Within a few days of being home, Jay was scheduled to be released. It turned out that he wasn't going to be there very long at all. Upon hearing that I was fearful, and I questioned my decision to not press charges. I grabbed Bruce and went a couple buildings over to a coworker's apartment. I told her that Jay was released and heading back home and that I was nervous of being home alone. I knew then I had made a huge mistake.

Several hours later, while at Chelsea's house, there was a knock at her door. It was Jay. Without me even telling him, he knew where to find me. His face looked just like the one I had looked up at that night while I lay on the ground. He looked angry, strung out, and sick. I knew instantly that everything he said on the phone was a lie.

Ten minutes later, I walked back home nervously. I wondered how I could ever be naive enough to believe that Jay was going to stay away from me. Shortly after arriving back, Jay had told me that he wasn't ever leaving the apartment, and he threatened that if I ever ran away again, he'd find me. I knew this was true. I was more trapped now than ever before.

Another long, torturous week went by. I went to work each day, then came home to Jay forcing me to explain everything I did that day and every person I spoke to. He'd continue to ask me the same questions repeatedly, waiting for my answers to change. I suffered from horrible stomach pains each day and severe headaches. Soon he was throwing things at me and hitting me again. Some nights I'd come home, and he would be waiting on the couch for me to walk in the door. And the minute I did, the agonizing hours of questioning began.

Although I was scared of talking about what Jay was doing, I decided to speak up. By this time, Lauren had become a close friend of mine. For a long time, she had been asking questions about Jay and life at home, and even though I never told her anything, I knew she was on to me.

So I decided to open up to her. I kept the worst details to myself, but I began to tell her more than I had told anyone else at that point. She was concerned for my safety, but I asked her to not involve the police. I promised her that I would do that, just not yet. I was taking a portion of my tips and hiding them under the mattress each day so I would have money for things I'd need in order to leave again.

It pained Lauren to hear about the things that had been happening, and she made me promise to call her if I needed help.

Over the following weeks, Lauren regularly checked up on me, and in her private time, she prayed for me and searched for ways that she could help me. She pleaded with me to go to the police, but eventually, she understood that I was terrified of doing that. However, after several more weeks of mental and physical abuse at home, I agreed to go to a local women's shelter. Lauren immediately contacted them and arranged for them to take me in the following day.

The next morning, I went to Kathy's and told her about my plan to go to a women's shelter for a few days until I figured out another plan. She called her daughter and son-in-law, who happened to live in the same apartment complex, and asked them to help me by giving me a ride. Shortly after, Melissa and Jonathon met us at Kathy's apartment. The plan was that I would go back up to my apartment and grab clothes while they waited downstairs in their car. Then they would drive me to Lauren's house. Jay was gone that morning, so this should have worked perfectly. However, as I came downstairs with my things, Jay had just arrived back. I could hear him yelling at Melissa and Jonathon. Soon, there was screaming, and Melissa was shouting for me to hurry and get in the car. Jay screamed at them for getting involved and stood in front of the car so we couldn't leave. We were facing a dead-end so Jonathon put the car into reverse and stepped on the gas. But before we could get away, Jay used his fist to punch in their driver side door. Jonathon quickly sped off, and we all watched fearfully as we drove through the complex, knowing there was only one exit to get out. Thankfully, we made it out before Jay got to us again, and I was taken to Lauren's house.

Later that day, Lauren and I arrived at a large, beautiful home in the nice part of town. Pink rose bushes lined the path leading to the door, and across the street was a park where kids played and dogs ran around. I felt hopeful that I would find rest here.

We walked inside, and Lauren spoke to the receptionist for me. I was given paperwork to fill out, and once I was admitted and the process was completed, Lauren said goodbye. She promised to visit me the next day.

A counselor welcomed me and invited me on a tour through the home. She showed me my bedroom, the bathrooms, and the phone they provided downstairs. It was a payphone with a blocked number for our safety; for anyone receiving a call from this phone, the number would appear as "unknown."

As I walked through the hallways, I passed by women who shared a similar story to mine. There was a woman, who appeared to be upset, speaking on the payphone downstairs, and several women were talking to one another in the kitchen. They looked at me, then looked away. None of the women smiled or said hello, and as inviting and comfortable as the shelter looked, it suddenly felt cold. But it was a place that I could get rest and a place where I was safe. I was grateful.

During my second day at the shelter, Lauren came back to visit. We sat out on the front porch and talked. Within a few minutes, she had told me that although she tried to convince the general manager otherwise, he decided he had to let me go. I was missing too much work. As heartbroken as I was, I understood.

But by the end of that day, the shelter was no longer a place of refuge for me but torment. Shortly after Lauren left, I decided to call Jay from the payphone and tell him I was in a safe place, but that I wasn't coming home. He had warned me to never run away again, and I did. I thought the longer I stayed away without him hearing from me, the angrier he'd become. Therefore, the more violent he would be the next time he saw me.

"I'm just calling you so that you know I'm safe, but I'm not coming home. You need to find somewhere else to stay."

"You're at a guy's house, aren't you?"

"No, I'm at a shelter. That's all I'm telling you."

"Sure you are." He laughed. "Oh, and by the way, I'm not goin' anywhere."

"That's my apartment, Jay."

"I'm not leaving!" he shouted.

I hung up the phone and walked away.

I got to the top of the stairs, and the phone rang. The woman that was on the phone earlier picked it up.

I stepped into my bedroom and lay on my bed. I could still faintly hear the woman's conversation.

"You wanna talk to her?"

I sat up, suddenly suspicious. Then I remembered that the number was blocked and there was no way it could be Jay. I lay back down. Moments later, it was quiet, and I didn't hear the woman saying anything.

Curious, I got up and peeked downstairs. She was still standing there on the phone. She looked up at me, then turned away.

I couldn't shake my paranoia. I went to my room and then waited to hear her hang up the phone.

"Okay, well you can call back and talk to me again if you need to," I heard her say. Then she hung up.

I waited a minute, then I walked downstairs. It was quiet, and I didn't see anyone. Then I walked toward the kitchen. As I approached the door, I heard the woman talking. "Yeah, apparently she's been sleepin' around. Poor guy said he's been so upset, and I guess she don't wanna talk to him. He said he's got no one to talk to so he started talkin' to me."

It *was* Jay that called, but how?

I turned the corner and looked at the woman who answered the phone. She stood in a circle with several other women. They all stopped speaking and looked at me.

I felt betrayed by these women. We all knew we were here for the same reasons, and despite being strangers, I expected as women we'd stick together. I looked at the woman, then walked away.

I walked to the receptionist desk. "You told me this phone number here is blocked, and it isn't."

"What do you mean?" she asked.

"The guy I'm here hiding from just called me back."

"Hmmm, that's odd," she said, confused. "I'm not sure why that happened, but I'm very sorry about that."

"He's calling here and talking to a woman here about me. That's not okay!"

"Miss, I don't have an answer for you. I'm very sorry."

I walked away. As I was walking up the steps, the payphone rang again. The same woman quickly ran to the phone. I knew it was Jay calling again. I went into my room, shoved my clothes into plastic bags, and then walked out.

The sun was setting, and I had no plan as to what I was going to do or where I was gonna go. I walked about a mile up the road to a payphone. With the small amount of change I had in my pocket, I called the church.

There was no answer. I wasn't surprised; it was getting late. I had nowhere to go so I sat by the phone with my bags until I figured out what I would do. For some reason, I decided I'd call the church again; this time, someone picked up.

"Hi! Can I speak to Pastor Flores?"

"He's unavailable. Can I take a message?"

"I need his help. When can I call back?"

"Uh, well, he'll be back here in about thirty minutes. You can try then." I hung up the phone and sat back down on the curb.

It was getting dark, and I had no way to tell what time it was. I waited for what I thought was thirty minutes and called back. Pastor Flores picked up. I was so relieved. I explained to him the situation and how I couldn't go home. He told me he would make some phone calls to see if someone could help me. He told me to call him in twenty more minutes.

I sat on the curb, watching cars drive by. It was now dark and getting cold. I hoped I had given him enough time, and I called back.

"Pastor Flores, it's Jessica. Were you able to get in touch with anyone?"

"Hi, Jessica. Yes, I have a woman named Theresa Carrillo who is going to come get you. She said you can stay with her and her family for as long as you need to."

I was overjoyed.

"Thank you, pastor!"

"Of course, Jessica. I am very concerned for your safety. You should not be with this man if he is hurting you. You cannot put yourself in this situation again."

His tone was serious, in a way that I had never heard before. It made me feel ashamed of myself. I knew he was right, but no one understood how terrified I was of making the wrong move or getting Jay arrested. Leaving him sounded easy, but it wasn't. And besides worrying for my safety, I was scared of losing everything I had worked for. I was desperately clinging to whatever I could keep.

For the next forty-five minutes, I waited in the empty shopping center parking lot, sitting on the curb next to the payphone. With every new set of headlights that drove past me, I wondered if it were them. Then, finally, a shiny red truck pulled up to me. A Hispanic man eagerly hopped out.

"Jessica! Hi. We're here to take you home with us!"

He was friendly and welcoming. He opened the door to the back seat where their two daughters were sitting. They looked just as nervous as I was.

"Hi, Jessica," Theresa said to me in her broken English.

"Hi. Thank you for doing this for me."

I would quickly find out that Theresa didn't speak much English at all, and her husband Manuel would do most of the interpreting for us.

When we arrived at their home, Theresa had a bed ready for me in my own room. I was so thankful to have my own space to think, pray, and cry. I was shown around the house and told to help myself to anything I wanted or needed. I thanked God with all of my heart for putting me here with this family.

That night, I climbed into bed, knowing I would be safe. I knew I could sleep through the night and wouldn't be woken up by Jay. I thanked God a thousand times that night. I was slowly making my way out of hell.

During the next few days, I spent a lot of time with Theresa while Manuel was at work and the kids at school. This was interesting since there was a language barrier between her and me, but we had fun with it. We tried to teach each other words in our own language, and many times it resulted in us laughing at one another. She was sweet, and she cared for me like she was my own mother. Each morning, she and I would get up at 4:30 a.m. and go to church for the 5:00 a.m. prayer.

When we walked into the church, it was dark and cold, but I was happy to be there.

After one hour of prayer, we would go back home, and she would prepare breakfast for us, and each night, she'd make us all a large dinner. I was grateful.

The Carrillo's had a way of making me feel at home and as if I were part of the family. I was sure by now I would've been anxious to leave, in fear of being in the way or a burden, but they did everything they could to make sure I didn't feel that way.

Chapter 45

After staying with the Carrillo's for about a week, we decided it would be a good idea for Theresa to come with me to the apartment to get some clothes. More than anything though, my heart was aching to see Bruce. Early the next morning, Theresa and I drove over to the apartment. She knew Jay could be dangerous, but she showed no fear or hesitation. Her confidence was contagious, and as I walked up the stairs with her, I felt safe. We reached my apartment; I unlocked the door and led the way as we stepped inside.

There Jay was, hovering over the kitchen sink. He flashed me a taunting smile before noticing Theresa was standing behind me. In Jay's hand was a lighter, and in the sink in front of him were ashes from the dozens of blouses, jeans, and bras he had burned. The counter was blanketed in ashes.

The three of us stood silently. I looked around and saw that large letters had been spray-painted all over the walls. The capital letters made out the words: "WHORE" and "I HATE YOU." Every wall in the apartment was covered in words. "SLUT" was painted above the couch, and "LIAR" was on a wall down the hallway. Where there weren't words spray-painted, there were large holes punched through the sheetrock. The window blinds were ripped off and lay on the floor. Burnt photos of Jay and me covered the floor along with scattered pairs of my underwear and other items of clothing. Every bit of clothing I had was now ripped and charred. The bathroom door hung off the hinges while the bedroom door had a large hole punched through it. The apartment was ravaged. No repair I could make would fix what he had done.

Jay didn't say anything to me; I sensed he felt uncomfortable that Theresa was witnessing all the damage he had done to the apartment. Theresa didn't speak a word. She stood in the living room, taking in the words painted on the walls.

Most of my things had been destroyed so there wasn't anything worth taking with me. Instead, I held Bruce close for a minute. He seemed happy and content. Despite the incident a few weeks prior, Jay usually played with Bruce and was gentle with him. I held him close for a moment and promised him I'd be back soon, and we left.

I was glad that Theresa saw what she did. I needed someone to see what I was dealing with. Up until that point, no one knew the severity of his mental illness, and he was always on his best behavior when others were around. This time, he was caught red-handed.

The ride back was quiet. I could tell by Theresa's expression that she was stunned by what she had seen. As I looked over at her during the drive, somehow I knew she was praying. She was praying for me and for Jay. Anyone who saw what she had would understand that this was serious.

Over the next couple weeks, I continued to live with the Carrillo's. Theresa and I had developed a close relationship, and I felt comfortable there. But it had been weeks since I had a job or a car, and I was fed up with being a burden on the Carrillo's. I was tired of not having my independence or seeing my dog. I knew I couldn't live this way forever. My fear subsided and was replaced with anger. In that moment, I refused to live in fear any longer. I was going to stand my ground and take my apartment back once and for all.

I thanked Theresa and the family for all they had done for me, but I told them it was time for me to go home. I took the bus home the next day.

I walked up the stairs to the apartment, and something within me was different this time. I wasn't scared. I walked inside the apartment, letting the door slam behind me.

"Do not talk to me! Do not touch me! Do not even look at me!" I said to Jay. Then, I walked into the bedroom and played with Bruce.

Chapter 46

Within a couple of weeks, I had a new serving job at a restaurant in Brentwood. Jay stayed away from me and didn't touch me. I even had the keys to the truck again. I worked hard, hid my money under the mattress, and spent all my free time at home with Bruce. My only focus was on my dog and paying my bills.

Weeks went by, and Jay had left me alone. He even agreed to leave. He said he was lining up another place to stay. I was elated. I had stood my ground, and I was taking my life back.

But days after that conversation, everything changed. I got up for work, and as soon as I was done getting ready, I walked into the living room to say goodbye to Bruce. As I stood up to leave, Jay walked over to the refrigerator. He pulled out our gallon of milk, which I paid for, walked over to me, lifted the milk up, and poured it over my head. Milk dripped down my face and hair. From my shirt down to my shoes, I was soaked. I felt humiliated.

He looked at me and waited for my reaction: for my tears and my pain to show. I couldn't give him that satisfaction. I grabbed a towel, patted my face dry, kissed Bruce, and walked out.

As soon as I got in the truck, I cried. I cried the whole way to work, then I wiped my tears, said a prayer for strength and walked inside. When I got home that evening and lifted the mattress to hide my tips, I saw that every dollar I had worked hard to save was gone.

Over the past couple of months, Lauren continued to check on me frequently. And although I still wasn't telling her everything, she knew far more than anyone else. She cared for me, and she was patient. She let me know that whenever I was ready to open up about the truth, she was there for me.

But it was still hard for me to be honest about all that had happened. I had so much shame, and I felt that no one would understand how trapped I was or the fear that I had and why I felt like I couldn't leave. But eventually none of it mattered. Lauren had seen enough, and she was tired of my millions of reasons and excuses for why I wouldn't put an end to all this.

Lauren had become so worried for my safety that she took matters into her own hands. She went to the police station and reported everything she knew. She had been patient, waiting for me to step up and go to the police, but she finally realized I didn't have the courage to do that.

I was about halfway through my shift, when a young officer walked into the restaurant. He was Officer Lopez, and he said that he was responding to a report made by Lauren. We went into the back room of the restaurant, and he began asking me questions. As much as I wanted to tell him everything, I held back.

"I wish that I could tell you more, but I'm not ready, and to be honest, I don't have the rent money. He's supposed to give me some of my money back in a few days, and if he doesn't, I'll lose my apartment."

"Ya know, I can't help you if you don't tell me what's goin' on."

"I understand. I'm sorry."

"So you really have nothing to tell me? I came here for nothing?"

"I'm sorry, but I promise I'll speak to you after the first of the month after I've paid my rent."

The officer sighed. "Okay." Then he walked out.

I found out later that once he left, he called Lauren. Rather frustrated, he told her there was nothing he could do to help me, and that it was a waste of time for the police to try to get involved.

But me buying time only made things worse. Within one week of Officer Lopez's visit, I was so hurt and emotionally spent that I didn't care anymore what Jay did to me. I was ready to come forward. I called Lauren and told her everything that happened. Immediately, she picked me up and took me to the police station.

Over the next couple of hours, I was interviewed and had photos taken of my visible injuries. That evening, I was issued a restraining order. I knew this piece of paper wouldn't keep Jay away from me, and if anything, it would make him angrier, but it was all I had. I didn't see it at the time, but God had a plan.

That evening, the officers told Lauren and me that they were heading to my apartment to serve Jay with the restraining order and tell him to leave. So while this was being done, Lauren took me to get some food, and we waited for the phone call notifying us when everything had been done. But, instead, we received a phone call that would change everything.

We were told that two officers arrived at my apartment with a restraining order in hand. The first officer knocked on the door while the second stood next to him. Thinking that it was me at the door, Jay opened up. But as soon as he saw the two police officers standing in front of him, he slammed the door shut. Before he could get the door closed, the first officer threw his body into the door to make his way inside. The officers yelled at him to open the door as Jay struggled from the other side to close it. Just then, the officers rushed their way through the door into the apartment. Then Jay grabbed the first officer and began to strike him—again and again—without stopping. The second officer tasered Jay, but she said it had no effect on him. She didn't stop. She continued to taser him until finally Jay's body fell to the ground. He writhed and convulsed on the floor as the officers struggled to get handcuffs on him. He yelled and resisted as they held him face down on the floor. He struggled to get away until finally they got the handcuffs around his wrists.

It turned out that the officer who was attacked by Jay was quickly taken to the hospital for his injuries. This officer happened to be Officer Lopez, the one who came to the restaurant that day and left annoyed with me. He witnessed firsthand the monster that I experienced on a daily basis. After this, his perception about my situation changed completely. Days after being hospitalized, Officer Lopez made a phone call to Lauren.

"This isn't any normal case; in fact, this is unlike anything I have ever seen. I understand now why she's so scared to leave … I get it now."

For so long, it had felt like no one saw what I saw. That no one could really understand the level of bondage, fear, and torment I lived in. I had come to hate myself for what I had allowed to happen to me. I often wondered what was wrong with me and why I had become the scared, timid person I was. But he was right; this *was* different.

I empathized for what Officer Lopez had to experience that night in my apartment. I was certain that it was terrifying for both officers involved. However, I had come to be grateful for the outcome of it. Now there were enough charges to put Jay in jail for a long time.

In the middle of all this taking place, I ended up with a "Three Days to Pay or Quit" notice on my door. I knew there was no way I'd make the rent. And, even if I did, I'd be struggling to make the next month's. I couldn't live this way, and I knew it was time to finally let go.

With three days before my eviction, Lauren, and her husband Joe, invited me and Bruce to live with them. This was an answer to prayer; I'd now have a new, safe place to live while being able to keep my job.

I called my mother, and, for once, I had an honest conversation with her. The very next day, she called in sick to work and arrived at my apartment with a U-Haul. I remember answering the door and seeing her and Paul for the first time since coming clean about everything. I avoided eye contact as much as I could. My hair was still very short and couldn't hide the scratches and bruises on my neck. And although I wore a long-sleeved shirt, I was sure I wasn't fooling anyone about the bruises I was trying to hide. It was July, and the summer heat was in full effect. By wearing a long-sleeved shirt, I made it too obvious I was hiding something.

But, my mother and Paul were patient with me. They didn't ask questions, and they didn't stare at the black and blue marks that showed through my skin. They didn't act this way because they didn't care. They did this for the exact opposite reason. Despite their anger and hatred for Jay, they kept their feelings to themselves because they knew I wasn't in a place to talk about these things. They also knew I hated asking for help, and I didn't want to be pitied by anyone. They respected me and gave me the space I needed. And now, when I needed help the most, my mother was there. She took the time off of work and rushed to help me during one of the most stressful times of my life. She and my brother loaded up my entire apartment and garage for me while I went to work. They took care of everything for me, and the empty apartment where my life nearly ended was now a sign of a second chance.

Chapter 47

The first few nights living with Lauren and Joe were the strangest and scariest. I was scared of being alone or having downtime. I knew that, if left alone in the quiet, I would be confronted with my thoughts. However, I knew the longer I ran from them, the longer they would stay.

I spent many nights sitting on the floor of my bedroom, crying, bringing my mind back to the most painful moments so they wouldn't be able to haunt me anymore. I prayed every night, sometimes for hours, that God would somehow use all this pain for something good. That He would turn the first twenty-two years of my life into something beautiful instead of it all being a total waste.

Within two weeks, Lauren helped me get my old job back, and, within four weeks, I had two jobs. I worked long days and spent my time off with Lauren and Joe and their family. From the day I met Lauren's stepmom, Tara, she claimed me as her adopted daughter and took me under her wing. And Lauren's dad, John, would sit quietly at the kitchen table for hours listening to me as I shared stories of what I went through. I felt like I was part of a family.

Not long after the court dates began, I began receiving phone calls from a woman in New York. I didn't know the woman, but she was someone who Jay had been communicating with by letter while he was in jail. She insisted that a man like Jay wasn't capable of doing the things he was charged with, and she begged me to reconsider my choice to press charges. Jay seemed to have the same effect on people as my stepfather Todd did. Many people never thought he was capable of doing the horrible things he did.

After unceasing phone calls and voicemails from this woman, I notified the police involved with my case, and I changed my phone number.

I told those around me that I would never live my life in fear again but the truth was that, in a lot of ways, I did. The reality was that I had come far, but I still had much further to go. Each and every night, I experienced nightmares. Sometimes I'd wake up from one, only to fall asleep and start another. In the middle of the night, I'd often get up to check every window and door in the house to make sure they were still locked. When I would go places like coffee shops, grocery stores, and gas stations, it wasn't uncommon for me to experience panic attacks at the sight of a man who even slightly resembled Jay. People in my life at that time knew not to startle me or make sudden loud movements because it would undoubtedly put me into a state of panic.

I lived with anxiety and post-traumatic stress disorder. The countless concussions and beatings I endured left me with traumatic brain injury, along with injuries to my eyes, my neck, and several other parts of my body. I suffered from chronic stomach pain and headaches, occasional loss of sensation in my arms and fingers, memory loss, and other symptoms.

Over the next several months, I spent many days at the courthouse. I gave statements, attended court hearings, and had meetings with detectives and victim advocate workers. By my side, each time, were Lauren and Tara, fighting with me. Tara attended every court date she could and protected me like I was her own daughter. I'm sure my own mother would've been there for these court dates had I invited her to be or had I notified her of any of the upcoming hearings. However, I felt very vulnerable during this time and I wasn't comfortable with my mother seeing me like that.

The morning of my first court date, I was overcome with anxiety. My hands shook as I sat on the wooden bench, waiting to be called into the courtroom. This was the first time I would see Jay since before his arrest.

I kept my focus on the witness stand as I walked into the courtroom, and once I was seated, I kept my eyes on the attorney. I could feel Jay's hate for me. And I knew he wanted me to look at him, but I wouldn't. Several minutes into the questioning, there was a long pause. I chose this as the time I would finally look at him. The hate behind his eyes was stronger than I had ever seen before. He glared at me so intensely that, even without words, I could hear him screaming at me. He wouldn't take his eyes off of me, and I wouldn't take mine off of him.

"Excuse me!" Tara stood from her chair. "He can't look at her like that," she shouted from the audience.

The bailiff walked over and stood in front of Jay so he couldn't stare at me. From behind, Jay moved his head from side to side, trying to see around the bailiff until he was ordered to stop. I'll never forget the angry look on his face as he struggled to look at me. This would happen again at the next court date. This time, when he was ordered to stop, he began wildly writing words on the piece of paper in front of him.

At my side during all of this, I had Detective Freier, a woman who believed in my case and in me. No matter how daunting the process seemed, she encouraged me to keep going, and she assured me it would all be worth it. I wanted Jay to get the prison sentence he deserved, but everything involved in making that happen was so emotionally draining that some days I questioned everything I was doing. Having Detective Freier push me to not give up was what I needed. I resolved to attend every court date until it was finished.

God strategically placed strong and tenacious women in my life at that time. In every corner was Lauren; Tara; Detective Freier; and my mother.

During all of this, Mom had developed a close relationship with Lauren. Despite some progress she and I had made, I couldn't help but feel guarded around my mother, and I didn't feel comfortable talking to her about any of the things going on. So, when she wanted to know about the case, or how I was handling the stress of all of it, she called Lauren.

It wasn't easy, but after several months, we were finally approaching a conviction. Women from Jay's past were now speaking up after being contacted by the detectives working on my case. They shared that they had information on Jay that would be valuable to us. Soon, however, each of these women backed out, fearful that Jay would learn about their involvement in the case. Despite this, between the evidence of my case and with the charges against him for assaulting Officer Lopez, Jay was facing a ten-year sentence. My hope of starting my life over could now be a reality.

However, as more time went on, and the more the case got dragged out, deals started being made. Jay had been in jail many times before, and he knew how to work the system. With just days before our trial, one last deal was offered to Jay, and he took it. He knew they didn't want to take this case all the way to trial and that they would offer him a better deal right before the date.

Which they did. Jay would now serve only four years instead of ten. Still, I had four years to rebuild my life in peace.

After the sentencing, Lauren and I stayed in touch with Detective Freier, and I would learn that my case was one that she would tell others about. She said that seeing successful cases like mine were the reason she continued to do what she did. She would go on to share my story to victims of domestic violence that came after me as a way to encourage them during their own journeys.

In the following months, everything in life seemed new, like I was experiencing everything for the first time. And I was. I was learning how to live a normal, ordinary life, something I had never done.

I attended counseling sessions, and I made a commitment to make God the center of my life. Soon I began creating goals for myself. More than anything, I wanted to travel. And I never wanted to worry about how I was going to pay my bills again so I worked three jobs and went to school part time. And in my quiet moments, I read scripture and prayed. And even though there were so many uncertainties in my life at that time, I had a deep sense of peace that I had never had before.

Abruptly, however, a new wave of challenges would interrupt my entire life. I began experiencing more symptoms of post-traumatic stress disorder and, suddenly, I wasn't the person I was before. I was numb to everything and everyone around me. I didn't feel human.

Next came mood swings and extreme anger. This would happen randomly—sometimes in the middle of a shift at work or on the drive home. There were nights when I would get on Vasco Road, a dark winding road near where I lived, and I would drive as fast as I could, daring myself to drive my car off the cliff.

Until suddenly, I felt the gentle spirit of God bringing my senses back, and I would turn around and go home. Counseling helped this to not occur as much over time and eventually it stopped occurring permanently.

For a brief amount of time, I experienced depression and confusion. There were so many things I couldn't make sense of so I decided to quietly pull away from God. I didn't stop believing He existed—I just didn't know if He was truly good. So I stopped seeking Him and I told myself I could figure things out on my own. I even tried to stop praying to Him but I found myself in prayer constantly. It didn't take long for me to realize that although not everything made sense with God, even less made sense without Him. I continued my journey of healing with counseling, my church, and those that loved me.

With the second chance God gave me, I had so much I wanted to do with my life. I had so much gratitude for the life I once lived and the one I was living now. I knew there were so many people struggling and hurting. There were children that went to bed hungry and cold each night and who didn't have money for lunches or clean clothes. There were women in cruel and abusive relationships that had lost all confidence in themselves and didn't know how to leave. I knew what all of these things felt like. And I wanted to spend this life God gave me helping those that were hurting in whatever way that I could.

So, I started by becoming a volunteer at a homeless shelter and I organized toy and food drives for low-income families. I collected gifts for local foster care agencies so the children would all have something to feel special, and I brought new clothes to women in women's shelters so they would have nice things to wear.

I had an overwhelming desire to help because I knew what it felt like to have nothing and to feel alone.

Chapter 48

It was now 2012. Two and a half years had gone by, and my life looked very different than it once had. I was still on my journey of figuring out who I was and who I was supposed to be, but I learned that that was to be expected and could take a long time.

I developed lifelong friendships and was slowly letting my mother be my mother. I purchased my very first new car, and I was traveling often like I had always dreamed of. Despite all of this, fear of the future overwhelmed me at times when I thought of the clock ticking down the time until Jay's release. I wondered what I would do and where I would move to. Little did I know that the plans that I was beginning to make would be cut short.

Jay wouldn't serve four years in prison. Instead, he was released after serving two and a half. The news came as a shock to everyone involved in my case. Upon finding out, I slipped into a paralyzing fear and panic and was inconsolable for several days. I questioned how this was possible. Myself, my mother, Lauren, and Tara were all registered on the inmate release notification list. This meant that each one of us was to receive a phone call notifying us if, and when, Jay was released. Despite this fact, not one of us received the call.

Over the course of the case, my mother's worry had caused her to make calls randomly to the prison to see if Jay had incurred any new charges and to ensure his release date was unchanged. If it weren't for my mother doing a random check, none of us would have known that Jay was released.

The days following the news, everything changed. At the same time I learned Jay was free, I had also learned I'd need to find a new place to live—Lauren and Joe had longed to start a life in southern California and although the timing was unfortunate it was time for them to move. I felt overwhelmed. My life was here and all three of my jobs were in the same city where Jay was coming back to. I didn't feel safe. It felt impossible for me to live my life normally if I was going to be constantly looking over my shoulder. I struggled with intense fear but also anger because I didn't want to live my life that way.

I realized that during the time I needed faith the most, I had abandoned it. I thought faith in God and peace beyond my understanding was going to be given to me. What I hadn't yet learned was it was a choice I had to make. I had to exercise this faith, not passively wait for it. If I truly believed God was all He said He was, I had to move forward and place my trust in Him. So, I tried my best to do that. Anytime the fear began to overwhelm me I asked Him to protect me and give me wisdom so that if I was supposed to move away or do something more to protect myself I would know that. After some time, I felt open to what plans God had for me, but deep down, I didn't feel that I needed to leave behind the life I had carefully built. So, I stayed. I kept working, kept showing up, and tried to carry on with some sense of normalcy. But that didn't stop the fear from creeping in during the quiet hours of the night.

Knowing Jay was still out there somewhere was unsettling—terrifying at times. I knew that if I didn't stay anchored in my faith, that fear could easily consume me or drive me to act impulsively out of panic. Each day, I had to bring those thoughts to God—sometimes over and over again.

Within a week, I had found a new place to live. Monica—once the friend Jay had forbidden me to see—had become one of my dearest friends. Her family welcomed Bruce and me into their home, and we moved in with gratitude and relief.

A month and a half had passed, and just as I was beginning to settle into my new home, I didn't know that my life was about to change in a way I could never have imagined. It was a Sunday night, and I was serving at the brewery. I felt my phone vibrating in my apron so I checked it and saw that Ron was calling. I declined it and planned to call him and Mom back on my break, but that's when I noticed I had over a dozen missed calls. Calls from Ron and Ron's family.

I asked someone to watch my tables for a second so I could step outside. I ran out to the back patio and called Ron. The phone rang for only a second before he picked up. There were no words on the other end, only the sound of crying.

"Jess," Ron cried.

"What's wrong?" I asked. My entire body began shaking in fear of what he was about to say.

"Your mom's gone. She's died, Jess."

My body went weak. I fell against the building behind me, and I slid to the ground.

He began to tell me that the two of them got into a heated argument the night before. Mom left the house that evening and never made it back home. The next morning, her car was found in a rural area, near the orchards. The car had been burned to the ground with her in it.

I was silent. Ron spoke, but I heard nothing. Instead, my mind played images of what had happened to my mother.

"I have to go," I said softly, then I hung up.

I stood up and walked back into the restaurant. I stepped into the side station while servers went back and forth around me, getting drinks and inputting orders. I stood there and stared blankly at the wall.

"My mom died," I began to say under my breath. A coworker stopped to look at me.

"My mom just died," I said again, as if this reality was now starting to hit me.

Another coworker standing near heard what I was saying and looked back at me.

"My mom just died." He quickly grabbed my hand and led me outside to the patio. A minute later, the manager was outside with me. I handed over my open tickets and all the cash I had collected that night then walked to my car. I sat in my driver's seat and wept.

I spent the days that followed in a depression that I believed would never go away. And, in the weeks to come, Paul and I were meeting with an attorney to search for answers in my mother's death.

Mom and I never had the normal mother-daughter relationship, even though, deep down, we both longed for that. We never enjoyed things like shopping together or talking on the phone about life, relationships, or anything remotely personal. But we had just reached a point where those things finally seemed attainable. My mother was sober, and she was committed to being the best version of herself that she could be. She had come a long way. And although decades of drug use took its irreparable toll, she had tried her best. She made amends for every hurtful thing she had ever done. She volunteered her time sponsoring and encouraging other women in rehab and she had many that looked up to her. She told people about God's love for them whenever possible, and she never judged anyone for their past. She had lived a hard life and had made many mistakes, but she knew God had forgiven her. She encouraged others with this truth.

I was proud of my mother, and I rejoiced knowing that she had come to find the love and validation that she had searched for her entire life. I was blindsided and devastated by the loss of her, but I knew she was finally set free from the bipolar disorder and depression that never let her out of their grip.

For months after my mother's death, I went to sleep at night only to be woken up from nightmares of her screaming as she burned in her car, crying and begging me to help her. At the same time, I still experienced the occasional panic attack and nightmare that Jay was going to come after me. The toll this all took caused me to take a step back from pursuing answers in my mother's case.

It's hard not understanding what really happened that night, and Paul and I each live with our regrets. The night my mother was in her car, right before it burned, she called Paul, but he missed the call. And three days prior to her death, my mother called me, but she called because she and Ron were fighting. She was angry and cursing and emotional. I didn't want to hear it so I told her I couldn't talk. She screamed at me over the phone and promised to never bother me again. That was the last time I ever spoke to her.

After our mother's passing, Paul and I truly only had each other, but that was all we needed, and that was kind of how it always was anyway. Paul and Mom were close though, and he loved her more than any son could ever love his mom. He respected her for all she had been through and all the work she was doing to better her life. I was happy that they had become so close, unfortunately, it was never as easy for her and I.

I do wish I had my mother so we could try again. I've thought about all the events in my life that she would miss: having children of my own and how they would never know their grandmother. I thought of all the things she wouldn't be there to see, but I also thought about all of the little things I couldn't do like call her or see her during the holidays. A dear friend of mine has always said, "Time relentlessly moves on," and she's right. Time doesn't take into consideration what you may or may not be ready for. It just keeps passing you by—relentlessly, carelessly. And as the months pass since my mother's death, I find myself caught between grieving what never was and letting go of what will never be. Her absence stirs up unanswered questions yet also invites me to heal in ways I never could while she was alive. Time has given me space to begin sorting through the grief, the memories, and the hope that somehow, I'm being remade in the process.

Epilogue

I wake up to a fresh cup of coffee that's been quietly placed on my nightstand by my husband. David thoughtfully leaves it for me knowing I'll be waking up soon. Behind my coffee is a photo of one of my most cherished memories—our wedding night. It's a black and white photo of him and me in the street in front of the old Sainte Claire Hotel. He was in his suit, and I was in my dress—an off-the-shoulder, vintage lace gown. As we stood in the intersection, David gently leaned me down for a dip, and our photographer caught the most beautiful shot. We stopped traffic for that picture.

I had always wondered how I would feel on my wedding day, without my mother or a father. But, as I looked around the room, I could see so many people who loved me, who, over the years, had supported me and who longed to see me happy. And I was. There was a time when I couldn't imagine peace—when chaos and pain seemed to be the only constants in my life. But today, I live a life I never could have fathomed. I'm married to a man who truly loves and respects me. He's kind, gentle, and steady—a reflection of God's mercy and grace in human form. My past doesn't scare him; he's a man who loves me for everything I am and everything I once was. Together, we've built a quiet, happy life, marked not by perfection, but by genuine joy and peace.

And we've created a family—something I never thought would happen, not because of inability, but by choice. I had fears about becoming a mother. I was terrified I would repeat the same painful cycles I witnessed growing up. I worried I would either love my children too much as some sort of unhealthy way to fill a void within me—or I feared I would not love them at all. I had no idea how to be a mom. When I found out I was expecting a baby girl, I went into a quiet panic. I lost sleep night after night, praying that the Lord would help me love her and be good to her because I feared I would be cold and distant. The idea of being tender and sweet with a daughter felt foreign to me. But day after day I asked God to lead me, to teach me how to be a mom. I wanted to love her in a way that was pleasing to Him. I wanted to love her the way He would. In my fear I chose to trust Him. And He so graciously answered my prayer. I love my daughter more than I ever thought I was capable of. I also understand that she's a gift from God and ultimately she belongs to Him.

We also have a sweet little boy who brings more joy to our lives we even thought was possible. He's our perfect little guy and he's made our family complete. My children are the crown of my life. Every time I look at them, I'm overwhelmed with gratitude that God would trust me to be their mother.

Motherhood has caused many moments of deep reflection on my own life and childhood. I didn't know what love looked like as a child, but now, I stand on the other side of that story. I am the mother now, and I have the chance to show my children what true love is—not just from me, but from their Savior. A love that is patient, kind, steadfast, and full of grace.

The Lord has taken me by the hand and walked me out of a life of pain and instability. He put my feet on solid ground. I now know that He had a plan all along. Every moment—yes, especially the painful ones—were known to Him. He never abandoned me. He was preparing my heart to understand what true love, grace, and redemption really was and He used my circumstances to draw me to Him, to show me His perfect love and sovereignty, and to make me more like Him. The more I grow in my knowledge of God the more I love Him. I know there's nothing I could have ever done to deserve the way He's loved me. My past grieved Him but He waited for me. I was His lost sheep. He is everything He says He is, and I entrust my life to Him daily. My peace is no longer circumstantial—it's rooted in Christ, and it surpasses all understanding. I may spend many more years bringing old wounds to the Lord for healing and that's okay. Because God is bringing my pieces together in a way that makes sense. And so I look to the future, not with fear, but with immense hope and excitement for what's ahead. The story isn't over yet—but now I know the Author, and I trust Him completely.

Abide with me: fast falls the eventide;
the darkness deepens; Lord, with me abide.
When other helpers fail and comforts flee,
Help of the helpless, O abide with me.
Swift to its close ebbs out life's little day;
earth's joys grow dim, its glories pass away.
Change and decay in all around I see.
O thou who changest not, abide with me.
I need thy presence every passing hour.
What but thy grace can foil the tempter's power?
Who like thyself my guide and strength can be?
Through cloud and sunshine, O abide with me.
I fear no foe with thee at hand to bless,
ills have no weight, and tears no bitterness.
Where is death's sting? Where, grave, thy victory?
I triumph still, if thou abide with me.
Hold thou thy cross before my closing eyes.
*Shine through the gloom and **point me to the skies.***
Heaven's morning breaks and earth's vain shadows flee;
in life, in death, O Lord, abide with me.

Henry Francis Lyte
1847

www.ingramcontent.com/pod-product-compliance
Lightning Source LLC
Chambersburg PA
CBHW021938290426
44108CB00012B/888